Much Love To You Mama

Ilamani Lafayette Hampton - Murphy
October 1, 1974 – August 10, 2011
In God's Care

In God's Care

By Evelyn Murphy

ISBN - (10): 0 - 985369604
ISBN - (13): 978-0 - 985369606
Copyright © 2012 Evelyn Murphy

For Questions, Comments or Concerns please write:
Overflow Publishing
P.O. Box 34815
Detroit, Michigan 48234

For additional copies of this book please contact:
Overflowingpublishing@gmail.com

Printed in the United States of America

The Life and Death of a Mother's Child

In

God's

Care

God's favor: For a grieving mother after her son was shot down in the streets of Detroit, Michigan by his so called longtime friend.

Evelyn Murphy
Overflow Publishing@gmail.com

Ratings

This book has been read and rated as five stars.

By: Pastor Joyce Jackson

I have never been so blessed and encouraged in the Lord, as when I read "In God's Care." This book is such a wonderful testimony of God's grace, blessing, and restorative power. I know it will bring healing to many families, as well as leading them to put their trust in God.

Mt. Ararat Freedom Gospel Church
Columbus, Ohio
Church Established in 1970
By the late: Reverend Nathaniel and Nancy Alexander

Pastor Joyce Alexander-Jackson has been the faithful daughter and through the passing of her parents. She listened to the Lord and heard His call and in 2001, she answered. Members come and go but the words of the Lord will stay forever.

In God's Care

This Book Belongs To:

Date of Purchase:

Notes:

_____

_____

_____

_____

_____

_____

_____

_____

_____

_____

_____

_____

_____

_____

In God's Care

In God's Care

Purpose

This book was written for believers and non-believers. It's not written to convince anybody about the power of God; it is written to tell you of His mercy and grace. We are all in the same body of Christ Jesus. Christ Jesus died on the cross for our Sins and rose on the third day so we can have eternal life. I'm writing this book to prove God is no respecter of persons. He has no favorites. He loves each of us equal. When we learn to pray faith filled words, we allow God to release His ability and take over the situation on our behalf. We are more than conquerors through Jesus Christ who enjoys working with us. God is still working miracles here on earth today. He lifted my soul and He placed a new heart in me at the altar. I'm living proof that miracles still happen here on earth today. We must trust, believe and have the faith of a mustard seed. This book will help non-believers, BELIEVE, and believers to become stronger in their faith. God is real and anybody can call on Him. There is hope in Him.

I hope this book will bless souls all over the world. I hope it encourages you to allow God to transform you into what He would have you to be. The stories in this book are true. God took me down memory lane to comfort me while grieving the death of my son. God placed this book in my heart to tell you the life of Ilamani (pronounced E-Money); my oldest son, who was gunned down in the streets of Detroit by his so called longtime friend. God clearly showed me that He has my son in His care. God told me that His ways are not our ways, when looking at E-Money or any other person He looked on the inner, and the outer. I knew E-Money's heart and how he often spoke highly of God. That was enough for me. How awesome is our God. God has truly blessed me. Now it's my turn to be a blessing to you. This book is for you and I'm sure it will help you understand God's amazing plan for your life. As you begin to read this book I pray for God to transform you into the person that He has destined you to be.

Take a moment before you start reading this book and ask God to transform you into your purpose. Remember our God has No favorites. He loves all of us equally and He is waiting on your call.

Dedication

This book is dedicated to you, you, and especially you. I'm truly grateful to our Lord Christ Jesus who is and always will be the head of my life. Much love, joy, peace, mercy, and grace to my late son E-Money, who was murdered on Wednesday, August 10, 2011 in the streets of Detroit Michigan. He will never be forgotten and will always be in my heart. To my wonderful, "God fearing parents" Luther and Claudia, they are still living, and in their 80's. To God Be the Glory. To my loving husband Leon for over 30 years, I deeply love, appreciate, and honor you. Thank you Honey, for your awesome love and your willingness you give so much. Much love to my beautiful daughter Kenyette, who has been my up-lifter and joy. My kind hearted son LaJuan, who God placed in my life as my light and my motivation. Thank God for LeShard, Kenyette's husband, Amber, LaJuan's fiancé, Leon Maurice my stepson, and my wonderful adopted daughter Rhonda who might not come when you want her but she's always on time.

To each of my brothers and sisters from oldest to youngest: Yvonne, Syria, Michael, Luther and his wife Carla, Titus and Cheryl, Louise, Nina and Ray, Ulysses and his fiancé Rhoda, and my youngest brother Todd, who all knows without God nothing is possible. I thank God that we have an unbreakable love for one another. To my nine grandchildren: Shavonte, she's the oldest and the controller, Ilamani Jr., he's the computer king, name it he can do it. Christopher the talker; there is power in the tongue. Sydnee the brain she's very intelligent and sweet. Azariah the beautiful one, she stays in the mirror and loves beautiful clothes. Emmanuel who's the loud one and he has a million dollar smile just like his daddy. LeShard the original crier; he cries to get his way. Serenity the sweetest, she's everybody's baby; her favorite words are pick me up. Last but not least my new born just three weeks old when his daddy was murdered; baby boy Kameron who was born July 21, 2011. He was a daddy's baby but now he's a mother's baby (smile).

To my Aunt Bessie of Macon, Georgia, and Aunt Jean of Cassopolis, Michigan. To my late Uncle Bro, Uncle Ellis, Uncle Charles, Grand Mother Flossie, Aunt Florence, Aunt Johnny, Aunt Nancy and Aunt Pee Wee. To my Mother-In-Law the late Ida Mae Wright who was a great woman of wisdom. She will never be forgotten we miss her dearly. May God continue to bless all my cousins, nieces and nephews. To Big Al who is a friend in deed and my so many friends that I just didn't have space to place their names.

Luther Hampton Sr. And Claudia Hampton
Cerebrating 65 Wonderful years of Marriage

Special Acknowledgement

If it wasn't for the love and support from Apostle Clarissa Dallas, and her ministering to me in the minutes, hours, and days after my son's death this book wouldn't be possible. Why? Because of her awesome teaching, she took time out of her schedule and stayed in daily contact with me until she felt I could be on my own. She also assigned an angel to watch over me. The angel was Minister Gwen Allen who has been under the leadership of the Dallas ministry for over thirty years. They followed the foundation that was laid out by the late Pastor Larry Dallas, husband of Apostle Clarissa Dallas and the father of Pastor Roderick Dallas. The love they have to offer is just in their blood and if you ever walk through the doors of True Gospel Tabernacle Church you would see what I'm talking about. I would like to acknowledge their great Sunday school classes that they have set-up for the beginners or the babes in Christ. The class is called the foundation class. It's the greatest class I could have ever attended. Sunday school classes are taught on every level from A-Z. Bible study classes are also available online and at the church every Tuesday starting at 12:00 noon and 7:00 pm. Apostle teaches noon classes and Pastor Roderick teaches evening classes with his wife Pastor L'aShawn. Their goal is to give the Lord's word to any and as many as possible. I would like to add in my own words, I truly believe in the Trinity. There is only one God who exists as three (3) persons; the Father, the Son and the Holy Spirit. They are the same in substance, essence and nature. They are different in person and in office. If I may say out of no disrespect to the Word or any religion or people Apostle Clarissa, Pastor Roderick and Pastor L'aShawn, they are truly my trinity here on earth. Three beautiful Pastors all on the same accord, serving together as one. I have served under their leadership for over ten years and as the song say: "I looked all over, still couldn't find no body." There's nobody better on this side for me. To all my Family members at True Gospel Tabernacle Church: Thank you for all your love, gifts, and great words of encouragement. Aunt Sis and Uncle Jr., Deacon Jones, Mother G. Micou, Mother A. Blackman and our late Mother Ruth Dallas. A special shout out to Pastor L'aShawn who I have served as her armor bearer for over seven years. I thank her for sharing her many gifts that God has placed in her. I truly enjoy walking and working with her. She is truly a virtuous woman and she wears the part of a first lady well.

In God's Care

Apostle Clarissa Dallas

Pastor Roderick & L'aShawn Dallas

To my true love friends: Aunt Joyce, Sister Barbara, and Judea (the greatest choir ever): Minister Jovelsa, Jessica, Kristy, Lauren and Brandon keep on allowing God to use you. Netta Powell, Elder Faye Bacon, Minister Helen Poellinitz, Tracy Hull, Pastor Tina, Pat Terry, Elder B. Lee, Minister L. Purry, Minister G. James, Lisa Graham, Minister Mary Davis, Deaconess J. Adkins, Nurse B. Robinson, and Deaconess S. Johnson. Thanks to my daughter Kenyette for being my personal dictionary and editor, along with my cousin Sonya Godbolt. Thank you sister Revie for formatting my computer into book form, making it easier for me to vision my book before I took it to be published. Special thanks to my neighbors and the men mentors that gave words of encouragement to my late son E-Money. My neighbor and friend, Joseph Vaughn who is a very positive man always helping and uplifting our young men. Two awesome men of God that have ministered to my son at alter call, Elder Brian and Elder Terry. A Super special thanks to the publisher Julius Justice of Urban City Publishing who encouraged me to go on with this book even when I knew no words to speak. I give thanks to God for giving me the strength, courage, and the words to write. Of course, my husband, Leon, who had to cook his own dinner many nights as I worked on my book. A pat on my own back for being obedient to God and hearing His call and submitting to that call with writing this book. I now have my own publishing company, Overflow Publishing. My second book is in production, "God Is Waiting". Again I say to you, you, and especially you. If I didn't list your name, and I should have, charge it to my mind and not my heart.

[13]

In God's Care

Contents
Introductions

In God's Care

Introduction

As I begin to introduce this book in the seconds, minutes, hours, days, and weeks of God's mercies and grace to a grieving mother after my first born of 36 years was gunned down in the streets of Detroit by a so call supposed to be long- time friend. What happened? Why? What could I have done to stop this from happening? Will I ever see my son again? What is he doing? Can he see or hear me? Is he Okay? Is he really at peace?

Questions?   Questions?   Questions?

Even as a Christian all these thoughts kept coming to my mind and running through my head. How do I help E-Money's children through this? How do I help my children through this? How does life go on after you lose a loved one? Who can I talk to other than God? Will this feeling ever stop? How can I be happy again? Will I stop crying in secret? What will I do in the courtroom when I see the murderer? What will he say? Will I ever know the real reason for my son's death? Was it jealousy?

Why?   Why?   Why?

Well here's one thing I do know. God can do anything but fail, so I'm going to trust in our Lord Jesus Christ to answer all these questions I have. I also know anything that Jesus starts He will complete. If you are reading this book and have lost a loved one, let the Holy Spirit which lives inside of you have His way. God is the only answer we have when troubled or overwhelmed, He will keep our mind in perfect peace, if we keep our mind on Him. Casting all our cares on our Lord Jesus Christ the Savior, remembering He is the way, the truth and the life. We must live on **(Proverbs 3: 5-6)** Trust in Him with all our heart and lean not to our own understanding and in all our ways acknowledge Him and He will direct our path. I must keep the scripture in my heart always. **My prayer to God is for Him to help me stand on His word, like never before. Help me God to set aside a certain time to praise you daily. Just being in your presence allows peace. In Jesus name I pray. Amen**

How One Telephone Call Can Change A Life?

Just hours after preparing for a good night's sleep, my life was changed by one telephone call. As I lay in bed I heard the phone ringing. I looked up at my clock, it was approximately 11:30 p.m. and it was at that moment I knew something was wrong. The feeling that went through my body was a feeling I wasn't familiar with. The first words that came from my mouth were, "Help me Jesus. Give me the strength I need to answer this call." When I picked up the phone, it was my youngest son, LaJuan on the other end. He said, "Mama, E-Money been shot, come now Mama he's here on Wexford." His voice was troubled and I felt his pain right through the phone. I knew at that very moment my son E-Money wasn't going to make it. I screamed with a loud voice, dropping the phone and looking for something to put on. My husband jumped out the bed and said "what's wrong honey? Who's on the phone?" I screamed from the top of my voice saying, "E-Money been shot, that was LaJuan. I'm going on Wexford." He tried to calm me down and get my attention, but I ran down the stairs and straight out the door, screaming and hollering.

My daughter lives two houses down from me so I ran to her house knocking, screaming and ringing her door bell. Her husband came to the door and she was right behind him. They asked me what was going on. While I was telling my daughter what happened, her husband LeShard ran to his car. I guess they were up watching TV, because they came to the door fully dressed. Her husband had to hear what I was screaming saying that E-Money had been shot because while screaming and telling Kenyette, my daughter, to come take me on Wexford, he was already at the car. Everything happened so fast. As we approached Wexford, I saw the street taped off and a lot of people, along with the ambulance and police cars. As her husband slowed to stop, me and my daughter jumped out the car trying to find out what was going on. As we started running toward the crowd we noticed two guys that we knew running toward us.

As they reached us they kept going. As they ran passed us I asked them where was E-Money and did he get shot. They kept running saying "yeah Mom." At the time, it didn't dawn on me why they were running away from the scene, I was just trying to see about my son. Later on that night I found out the reason they were running away from the scene was because their brother Boo, was the one who had murdered my son, E-Money. They had come back to the scene to find out what condition my son was in.

I then ran over to a police officer and asked him where was my son E-Money, explaining, "I'm the mother of the person that had been shot." Please help me, tell me what's going on, can I see him? At that point, I was asked to calm down. As I looked out into the crowd, I noticed the crowd of people looking at me like they were feeling my pain. I started screaming, *"Tell me somebody, tell me what happened to my son..."* Nobody said anything and I kept screaming, *"...please in the Name of Jesus, please tell me what happened to my son... My phone number is 313..."* and I shouted out my telephone number over and over and over. Meanwhile, I saw the ambulance just sitting there and I knew that if my son was going to make it or had a chance the ambulance would have been gone.

I went back up to the police officers and asked them could they please tell me the truth, was my son dead? They looked at me surprised and informed me to go down to Receiving Hospital and they would meet me there. They asked if I had a car or needed a ride. I found my daughter and her husband who had been asking questions to the crowd of people they knew. I told them what the police officer said so they dropped me off to my house so I could put on my clothes. They didn't wait on me they went straight to the hospital. I had ran out the house with my night clothes and my house coat. When I got to the house my husband wasn't there. I got my eye glasses, threw on some slacks and jumped in my van.

Driving to Receiving Hospital

My cell phone begins to ring. Call number one: Hi Mrs. Murphy. Boo shot Money. I said, "Hello, hello. What?" The caller repeated, "Boo shot Money." Then they hung up. I called to see where my husband was and he was on Wexford on his way to the hospital. On my way to Receiving Hospital I got about six calls from different unidentified people telling me who shot my son. One person was crying so hard saying, *"Boo shot Money and all Money was doing was telling him to put that gun up."* I kept asking who am I speaking with but they never answered. I knew before I got to the hospital that my son was dead. As I entered the parking lot of the hospital I could fill my son's spirit. I asked God to give me the strength I need right now for my family. Going through the doors of the emergency room and seeing my daughter fall to the floor I knew I needed God like never before. I started talking to God as I approached my daughter, saying the same thing over and over, "Give me strength Oh lord give me strength." The doctor, nurse, and two people were there with my daughter and her husband. I announced myself as E-Money's mother and they informed me of his death. My soul felt empty and my heart immediately got heavy. I knew this was just the beginning of a lifetime of emptiness. I also knew that I serve a God that can never fail and He will never leave me. As I proceeded to walk toward my daughter and her husband, the strength of the lord came upon me.

Mark 11:24
Therefore I say to you, whatever things you ask when you pray, believe that you receive them, and you will have them."
I began to pray; I had to focus myself on the Lord's promises. I needed the Holy Spirit to show up in me. This was an urgent matter and all I knew was to pray. I thank God for prayer, prayer changes things.

Leon and LaJuan Arrive Together

I began to worry about how I was going to tell E-Money's children. He just had a three week old baby boy. I knew that he wouldn't understand or know what was going on but he had five other children ages eighteen, sixteen, thirteen, seven and six, all who loved him and played a big part in their daddy's life. All I could say was, "God give me strength and please give my grandchildren strength." Leon and LaJuan came toward me and I felt myself getting weak instead of becoming strong. I noticed my grandson Chris exploding into an anger state. He was crying saying no and hitting the walls. Chris had just heard that his uncle had died. I knew I had to be strong for him. His uncle was like a second father in his life. I immediately went over there to him to calm him down. The doctors and nurses took him in a back room and called for a grief counselor, and asked all the family to come in just as Leon and LaJuan arrived. After talking to us, and explaining to us the cause of my son's death they asked us to call all family members that we needed to be with us and when we were ready they would take us up to identify his body. I never knew who called who all I knew was that when I looked around, more than half of my family members were there. E-Money was the first born out of over 40 cousins just in my family alone. His aunts, uncles, cousins, children, fiancée, friends all were there for support. When Leon and LaJuan arrived and all was ready we all went up to identify my son E-Money.

I began to pray in silent asking God for this to be a dream. It seemed so real and deep down inside I knew it was real, but I still prayed in silent for this to be a dream. As I write this book 30 days later, I'm still asking for this to be a dream. I know it's real, but a dream is what I would like it to be.

Identifying His Body

The staff at Receiving Hospital was great. They explained to us how my son died and told me that he had been shot five times, twice in his abdomen inches from his navel, and inches from the right side. The bullets penetrated through his liver and came out his back leaving four holes. He also was shot in his arm, leg, and upper back leaving a total of seven holes in his body. I wanted to faint, scream, run or do something. Just hearing about a person getting shot that I didn't know would have caused me to feel sad. But to hear this from a doctor about my son being shot five times with seven holes just ripped my heart right out. I had to be strong for my family. I wanted the God in me to show up now like never before. I needed God to help me help my family.

Seeing my daughter Kenyette and my son LaJuan cry and there was really nothing I could do; this was more than I could bear. This in itself, along with other occurrences in my life, was creating insurmountable problems for me. That problem is still with me today as I write this book. The first stage of grief is shock and emptiness. I knew what was going on but all I could think of was being strong for my family. Little did I know I was about to lose my mind with uncontrollable emotions that came out of nowhere. While going up on the elevator to identify my son, I begin to feel light headed and overwhelmed with pressure. Everybody was crying and holding on to one another. My husband was walking with me and I was doing fine until I saw my baby's body through the big glass window. He looked as if he was at peace, but I couldn't take another minute of being silent. The bomb exploded in me and I lost my mind screaming rampantly. That feeling was something I couldn't control. I could see everybody around me and what was going on but couldn't pull myself back to reality. I saw my husband, kids, family and hospital staff there and I was trying to pull myself together, but I was overcome with emotions, still wailing in disbelief. I remember being placed in a wheelchair and trying to get back there to my son but all I can remember after that was my husband putting me in the car. How I got back on the elevator, to get down to the parking level I don't remember. I do know that state of mind was a place that I never want to be or experience again. My granddaughter Shavonte was E-Money's oldest child and she was taking it just as hard as I was. I couldn't get to her to help her because at the time I couldn't help myself. Her mother Wynnie was there with her, so I knew she was in good hands. I saw my daughter Kenyette and my son LaJuan standing in a state of shock. I thank God for my husband Leon as he took full control of the situation along with my brother Luther. They were informing everybody to leave the hospital parking level and meet up at our house. My sister in law Carla drove me home, as Leon and her husband Luther followed in their cars. My mind was wondering in all directions, I didn't know what to do or what to say. I could hear my sister-in-law praying as she was driving me home. My head was hurting and I had a lot of questions. I just had to scream out loud asking God why? Why God Why? Why my son? **Then out of nowhere came**

Matthew 5:4
Blessed are they that mourn: for they shall be comforted.

Jeremiah 31:13
For I will turn their mourning into joy, and will comfort them, and make them rejoice from their sorrow.

God speaking to me in scripture happens to me often as I walk in His word. This was something much bigger than big to me and I didn't understand what to do or how to act. All I wanted was my son. I knew God was with me, but why did something like this have to happen to me.

My prayer was for God to carry me day by day and teach me how to get through another day with my mind never leaving His presence.

How am I Feeling?

Upon arriving home from the hospital I felt like my life was over. I couldn't look at my husband, daughter, or my son LaJuan in the face. I felt so helpless. My love for living was over. I felt like my insides were being snatched out and there was nothing I could do about it. It seemed that this was going to be a long night. All my family members were coming in one after another. Before long, the night had turned to early morning. I was tired but sleep was not on my mind. Not only was E-Money my oldest son, he was my biggest reason for praying and serving God the way I do. E-Money believed that all his blessings came from God because of me praying and always talking to him about right and wrong. He kept me motivated in doing God's work. If I said or did something that wasn't Godly in front of him he would say with a big smile on his face, "all right mama God heard that." E-Money helped me to keep the God in me, even though he also brought the devil out of me sometimes too (smile).

I knew I really was going to miss my baby and I had a lot of questions for God. Should I ask him? Well, I thought to myself God knows what I'm thinking anyway, so why not. What am I going to do now? How can I live? I really don't want to live? What about Kenyette and LaJuan? What about My grandbabies? Oh God my husband has always helped me through any and everything, but this is something too big for him. God we all really need you now like never before.

My heart has no feelings, my mind can't think. How am I feeling? Words cannot explain. I'm lost in a body and I know not what to do. Everybody is trying to cheer each other up. How? We will never feel the same. I have always been a positive thinker, but only negative thoughts were coming to my mind. I seen my family falling apart right in front of my face and there was nothing I could do. I knew God could fix anything but at the time I didn't see this problem getting fixed. I just saw the sadness in my son and daughter. This was sadness that mama or daddy couldn't fix. My body was tired and I wanted to get away from everybody. Where could I go? I knew I couldn't go to sleep, and I didn't want to leave my husband and kids downstairs with all the company. So I suggested that everybody go home and try to get some rest and come back over in the morning. When I got up in the morning I was hoping for this nightmare to be a dream. But it was real and I knew that I must trust in God. How can I help my family through all this pain when I can't even help myself? My prayers must be filled with faith and trust. I know I'm feeling helpless and all alone, but I also know that I serve a mighty God so I'm going to put a smile on my face and let God keep working through me. It's not going to be easy but this is where I will start. I believe that God is going to get me and my family through this.

[23]

Thoughts Run Through My Head

I go to bed at night, wondering why you had to go. I believe in God and you do too. I can't help but wonder why He had to choose you. Your death was too fast. Your life was just beginning. Your death leaves nothing but a sad ending. Your death left a heartache that no one can heal. I can't believe this is really real. I can still feel your presence all around me. I just want to see you again. Knowing that you are gone I have to be strong. I know you know what's going on inside of me. I pray to God asking him to help the family get through this. I guess when you lose some one as loving as you, grief will always be there. I heard people say there's nothing too hard for God, and I know that's true, but when I look in the eyes of all the loved ones you left behind, I see the sadness and crying silently inside. I know this will never be behind us but I'm asking God to show us how to deal with it. I love you so much E-Money and I always will. Having to realize you're not here takes me to a sad place, a place that I can't understand. I know that I can carry you in my heart. That sounds good and that's what I'll do. But it's hard for me E-Money because I really miss you. Here's something no one can steal, the love we shared here on earth. I can hear you singing two of your favorite songs. Going Up Yonder and We Are Family. I'm going to keep those songs in my heart as I vision you singing, so until I see you on the other side, peace to you, my first born son and my lifetime friend. Mama

God is good and His mercy endures forever. I pray that I see my son again. God you have shown me that my son is in your care. Keep me living upright so I may see him again. In Jesus name I pray.
Amen

Preparing My Son's Funeral

I knew everything about preparing a funeral. I had helped many family members and friends with funeral arrangements in the past. I never ever thought this day would come for me to bury my son. It's a hard place to be but because I believe and trust God, as I do, I knew I could handle it. I knew that my son's funeral would be held at my church, True Gospel Tabernacle, where I have attended and been a member for over ten years. I attended faithfully and was very active as an armor bearer. Wherever they needed me to be, or whatever they need me to do I did or was there. True Gospel Tabernacle Church is my life. The Pastors are individuals after God's own heart, and that is what they teach. My son attended there off and on whenever he went to church. He believed in our Lord Jesus Christ as his savior and he would call me daily on his way to work for prayer. So I knew his funeral would be at my church.

I had a girlfriend who worked at Barksdale Funeral Home and I knew she would take care of whatever had to be done for the viewing of my son's body. While thinking of all the things that had to be done before the funeral, I begin to feel overwhelmed. I wasn't going to allow Satan in this time. I called on God and all I could say was help me God. My mind wouldn't let me say anything except help me God. I tried to pray but the only words that came out of my mouth were, help me God. I didn't know what color his suit would be, nor did I know what color the casket would be, or where the people would go after the funeral. I didn't know who would do the cooking. My family and friends said they would handle everything but I felt clueless. I wanted everything to be perfect and I needed some help. Then the doorbell rang. It was my Apostle Clarissa. She was there to tell me just what I had been worrying about. Look at how God works. She said that the church would buy, cook, and serve all the food after the funeral. What a big relief. God had sent an angel to my rescue. God was preparing my son's funeral for me. She prayed with me and answered some questions that I needed to understand about death. She stayed over and I could feel the anointing all over my house as she just sat there and smiled. I could see God working it out already on my behalf. The following night as it got late and time for me to go to bed again I couldn't sleep. I tried hard but all I could do was toss and turn all night. My husband Leon tried to comfort me in every way, but there was nothing he or anyone could do. At about 5:00 a.m., The Lord began to speak to me. He showed me my son, E-Money, in a white and gold casket, white suit, with a white shirt and gold tie. I jumped up out the bed, because it was so real. When I got up and realized what had just happened I began to praise God like never before. I also saw a big silk banner over his casket that said, In God's Care. It had to be about 7:45 a.m. when I looked at the clock. So from 5:00 a.m. to 7:45 a.m., I was in God's presence and He gave me the instruction and vision on how to bury my son. Don't you know I will never stop praising and loving my God. This was enough for me to just be at peace. I wish it could be that easy. I had to go to the morgue to re-identify E-Money's body so he could be released to the funeral home. My friend Tina, who is a pastor, came along with me and my family. After going down to have my son's body released to Barksdale Funeral Home, we had to pick out the casket and a date for the funeral. I thank God every day for my brothers and sisters support that day. They stayed with me at the funeral home until everything was finalized. The vision that God had given me about the casket's color and the writing above the casket in silk and satin that read; "In God's Care" was just as I had seen in my dream. I hadn't had a chance to tell anybody because the day was moving fast, but when we got to the funeral home to pick out the casket, it was just as I had seen in the vision. My family and I handled all the necessities. When we left out of the funeral home everything was just as God had shown me. I began to rejoice in the Lord and my family kept saying how strong I was. I knew it was God's grace and mercy that was carrying me through.

Preparing for the Viewing of E-Money's Body

My husband and I had to bring everything that was needed for the burial to the funeral home. They asked if we had someone to cut his hair and shave him. We have several barbers in our family and he has a cousin Dee, who would cut his hair most of the time, and he knew the cut and shave that E-Money wore. So I asked Dee if he felt like he could handle that. He agreed and went and cut his hair. Dee and E-Money also hung-out together from time to time so that would also allow Dee his private time with E-Money. My husband and I went and picked out his suit and tie and to my surprise the first store we went to had exactly what I needed: the suit, shirt and tie all at one store. My son was ready for his home going and I was filled with praise. The suit was white and the tie was gold, just as God had shown me in my vision. God had handled everything for me and my heart was at peace. I wanted to shout out loud hallelujah! Right there in the store, but I knew people or my husband would not understand so I waited until I got outside near our car and said to my husband in a soft voice isn't God good, he said yes then I shouted out Hallelujah! Hallelujah! Look at how God is gonna bury our son.

I thank you God for all you do. I will praise you all the days of my life. I see the goodness of God all around me. I pray my faith in His word regardless of what my mind is thinking or how my body is feeling. I must keep on trusting in your words.

Viewing E-Money's body at the funeral home

My husband and I arranged to be the first to view our son's body. When entering the funeral home and seeing how natural my son looked and the peace on his face as he lay in his casket, we knew that he had to have come in contact with God before his death. He was lying in his casket with his arms and hands over his chest with his thumbs up. To me that indicated that E-Money was **In Gods Care.** I know God works in mysterious ways and I knew that was another sign from God to let me know my son was in His care. I remember just days after E-Money's death as I lay in bed crying and talking to God asking "why?" God showed me a flame of light and a picture with E-Money's face in the background and above E-Money's head read, **"In Gods Care."** Look at God's capability being released.

At the viewing, my husband and I began to pray to God for E-Money and thank God for the peaceful look on our son's face. Meanwhile, other family members began to enter the room. Our youngest son LaJuan and Amber entered first. Kenyette and her husband and children entered. Next E-Money children's along with his fiancé China. We kept praying until E-Money's oldest child Shavonte began to cry out for her daddy. At that point everybody in the room reacted in the same way. I allowed them their turn to cry out. After I began to explain to them what God had shown to me that calmed them down for a few minutes before they started again. E-Money's six year old son and seven year old daughter wanted their daddy to wake up. I remember telling them that their daddy was going to stay asleep until Jesus comes and take him to heaven. Manie, who is the six year old, said he wanted to go with his daddy. I told him not this time and his mother, Tawanna, picked him up and took him outside. The room was getting crowded and people were trying to kiss and hug him. I understood that he had a lot of love from many different people but at the same time I wanted him to stay clean free of any stains or tears on his suit. I asked the funeral director to rope off his casket. So when people come in they would see him but not touch him. When friends of his arrived, that I knew I explained to them my concerns and allowed them to go around the rope only if they promised to be careful. He had over 100 friends viewing his body, friends I knew and friends I didn't. I knew his funeral was going to be over packed because he was loved by so many. He shared his love with his friends just as he did with his family. After being there for about five hours and all his family members that I knew was coming to his viewing. I asked the funeral director not to allow anybody else in there. They agreed and we all left. It had been a long day for me and my husband so we went home. My son and daughter went to the fundraiser my brother Luther and other family members had set-up. E-Money's insurance had expired six months before his death and he didn't get a chance to renew it. His cousin Donte' and Rhonda along with others gave me a personal donation. The fundraiser was selling t-shirts with E-Money's picture on it and the other fundraiser was a barbeque at the park. I would like to thank everybody who participated.

I truly would like to thank God for my family and friends.

E-Money's Birth Father and Family Arrived

E-Money's birth father and his aunts, uncles, and cousins arrived in Detroit Sunday, the day after the family viewing. I asked the funeral director if they could make provision for a special viewing for his family on that Sunday to which they agreed. When they arrived in Detroit they called and I gave them directions to the hotel and to the funeral home. I told them to call me when they were on their way. It had been years since I had seen the family or talked to them. They never kept in contact with me or E-Money, although he kept in contact with them. He would go there every year to visit his cousins Vicky, Carla, Johnny, Tony, Longene and Earl. I can't remember all their names, but he loved them all, especially Althea, Neice and Sara, his aunts. He was planning his family vacation to visit them at the end of August as he had been doing for the last three years of his life. He was a family person. He loved his family in spite of. For them to be coming all the way to Detroit indicated to me the love they had for him also. It was an honor to see them and it was a great blessing all at the same time. I didn't get to say much to them but I did let them know that I appreciated them coming.

Preparing the Obituary

I have seen many different obituaries before and I knew I could just look at some old ones that I had and prepare E-Money's. Well I had been looking all that day and nothing seemed to satisfy me. Knowing that God is omniscient and omnipotent, I decided that if he prepared my son's funeral then He would prepare his obituary. I begin to trust in God again. I went to sleep that night and as I slept God gave me the most beautiful dream I could ever have. I saw my son in a new home with angels all around. The next morning when I got up I began to do his obituary. As I was working on it (obituary), the doorbell rang. It was my sister- in -law Joyce, with an obituary in her hand. A reading in the obituary tells of a change of address. I read it and as I did I allowed the Lord to minister to me more about my dream of my son's new home. Just look at God's Amazing Grace.

God gave me these words to write: From E-Money:

The Title: E-Money's New Address

Hey everybody:

Just want to let you know my new address. I received a call from God, the Alpha and Omega, the Beginning and the End, the finisher of my life, the King of Kings, the Lord of Lords and I can go on, but He informed me on August 10, 2011 that my new home is ready. He told me that His son Jesus paid the cost and I can move in immediately. My new home is so beautiful and a great sight to see. It is in an exclusive location and it is surrounded with beautiful pearl gates; and guess what? The streets are paved with gold and every day is the Sabbath. There's peace, love, joy, and happiness just floating around. There's no hurt, no pain or fear. Oh, wait a moment I have to go now and get fitted for my wings, but first let me give you my new address:

888 Heavenly Ave.
God's World, Jesus Town 77736

I don't have a telephone number yet, but you can call God. If you don't have God's number, He is listed in the Bible on every page. **Ilamani, better known as E-Money**

Now if that didn't make my day and help me through this; Check out what happened next? The number 8 means a new beginning. God is still confirming that E-Money is in His care. His new beginning is at his new address 888 Heavenly Ave. The number 7 means complete. E-Money has completed his life here on earth and will now complete his work in God's World, Jesus Town 77736 and 36 was his age when he was called home to perfection. Look at how God comforts and heals my pain. How many of you know that God has a great sense of humor. He will take you where you need to be taken. How awesome is our God.

Guess what! He didn't stop there. Later that day as I began to finish up the obituary so my cousin, Sonya, could type it out and print it. I needed help on some final arrangements and I didn't know what to do because it was getting late. Again my door bell rings and now it's after 8:00 pm. All my company was gone and my remaining family was preparing to leave. It was my Apostle Clarissa at the door coming to see if I needed any help with the obituary. See how awesome God is. I was so amazed at how God had me wrapped up in his mercy and grace. God had sent me an Angel right here on earth. Apostle was the Angel that God sent to me. She helped me to finish up the obituary. I had been praying all day back and forth wondering how was his obituary going to look or will he even have one. All I knew was to pray and trust God. That's all I had and really needed. At the time I didn't understand that. I wanted my mother; however I couldn't share my pain with her because she had been diagnosed with a severe case of dementia. Normally, she would be right by my side praying with me and helping me through this horrible nightmare.

I love the Lord with all my heart and I thank Him daily for my new family that He has placed in my life at True Gospel Tabernacle Church. As you see, God can do anything but fail.

The Morning of the Funeral

I had been so busy preparing for my sons funeral to be perfect, that I forgot to select something for me to wear. My husband, son, daughter, and grandchildren all were dressed and ready to go. I had taken my shower, decided on my attire, but I just kept on my long robe and nobody knew I wasn't dressed, because I had on my stockings and shoes. The limousine arrived and everybody went to the door ready to go. The limo arrived an hour early, so I had to run upstairs to get dressed. The limo drivers and my family waited until I was dressed.

At The Funeral

I entered the doors of my church the same as I had every Sunday for the past ten years. I walked through the doors Sunday after Sunday ready to praise and worship God, but now my son's funeral was being held there. That had to be the hardest and most traumatic thing I ever had to do. I really don't remember too much about the funeral because I was in total shock. I can say I felt the love and pain of the people who was in attendance. After finishing up all that was needed to give my son a proper burial, I guess I really didn't realize, that my baby was really gone. My husband had to help me walk in and sit down at the funeral. While sitting down right in front of my son as he lay in his casket, like many other mothers before me after losing a son, it took me to a lonely place. I felt like God had let me down? I lived my life praising and worshiping God and I prayed daily for the protection and safely of my children. I never prayed for fame and fortune. All I ever wanted out of life was to be happy and that my family stayed safe. I never felt so hurt and betrayed. I knew that my thoughts were out of order and needed to be checked. Who was I to feel betrayed and let down. I know that God is perfect in all His ways, but I was stuck in a place that only God could remove me from. I remember people coming up to me giving their condolences. I remember my son (LaJuan) just sitting right in the first row in front of E-Money's casket never leaving from beginning to end. I can only imagine what was going through his mind. They were two peas in a pod. The love they shared as brothers truly came from God. My daughter (Kenyette) was in a state of shock but she was trying to hold on for E-Money's children and her son, Little Chris. She had to be the "up-lifter" in the family during this time because I was down and she always had my back. I thank God for my strong daughter and son. Without their 100% support I couldn't have made it.

His funeral was packed wall to wall. In addition to the sanctuary being filled, people was standing in the hallway and outside because there wasn't any place to sit. My church is large with a balcony and seats over six hundred people. I was told that there were more than seven hundred family members and friends who attended. E-Money was very popular and known for the respect he had for his elders. I remember all the while that I was sitting during the funeral, trying to focus my mind on the service and the singing, people kept coming up to me saying how respectful my son (E-Money) was. That was a good feeling and when I would look up and see him in his casket lying so peaceful a small relief would appear. During one part of the service I remember hearing Minister Sheila sing, His Eyes Are on the Sparrow and then a great relief came over me. The second time I felt good at his funeral was when my Pastor, Roderick Dallas preached the Sermon for the service. I thank God for his many encouraging words. He is what you would call the top of the line pastor. He doesn't sugar coat the Word; he tells it like it is. He's young, handsome and a true man after God's own heart. I, serve as armor bearer for his wife, First Lady L'aShawn. I call her my personal angel sent from God to share life about becoming a real woman. She wears that role well. She's beautiful, not only in looks and fashion, but in her ways as well. God placed her in True Gospel Church to help to teach women how to be "a lady" along with all her other wonderful gifts. His mother our Apostle Clarissa; she "puts the sugar in the cake," she's the sweetest person you could meet. Now preaching and teaching God's word is her lifestyle. When I look at her I feel the presence of God; now isn't that awesome. Just to look at a person and see that the presence of God is all around them. To me this proves she's a mighty woman of God. I'm sure anybody that knows her will say the same. I thank God for them; they helped to make my son's home going a great success. I especially thank God for all my TGT family and a special "shout out" to Minster Sheila and Sister Earlene our personal song birds.

Driving To The Cemetery

My husband and I exited the church returning to the limousine. I began to realize this was it. I thank God every day for my husband. He took care of me as if I were a new born baby. He never left my side. I say "To God be the Glory" for a husband that has so much love for me and I feel the same in return. I'm now beginning to realize that I would not get another chance after today to say my goodbye. What a place to be in? What a horrible feeling? How do I make myself feel better? I see all the love around me, but I'm not feeling it at all. My pastors would always say, when preaching or teaching the word, that the devil sneaks his way in when we least expect him to. Once you catch on to his tricks it's easy to know when he approaches you. I knew I needed to hold on to God no matter what. I wanted so hard to be strong and fight the devil off. All I could think of was to pray. I knew if I prayed and resisted the devil he would flee. I began to pray out loud in the limousine. The limo driver was a lady. I didn't think about where I was or who was in the limo, I just began to pray. When I began to pray, she joined in. The love of God entered into my soul and peace rested on me. How awesome is our God.

When we arrived to the cemetery, my husband held me tight. As we walked my husband whispered in my ear, "God can fix it baby everything you ask Him He can do. Just hold on. I'm right with you." My husband tried to make things as easy for me as he could. I love and appreciate him for that. I just didn't know what to do or which way to turn. All I knew was to wait on God. That's all I knew. Through my tears, I looked up and saw the pallbearers carry E-Money to his grave.

At The Cemetery

Saying my last goodbyes to E-Money was the hardest thing I ever had to do in my life. I can't say it enough how I thank God every day for my Apostle Clarissa and my Pastors Roderick and L'aShawn Dallas. As they prayed his final prayer I felt the peace of God all around me once more. I begin to pray in silence as my husband Leon whispered in my ear saying, "you're doing good baby, I'm here, I'm right with you, stay strong."

After everyone had left, the cemetery, my children Kenyette, and LaJuan, stayed to grieve a little while longer. Rhonda, my adopted daughter, had a hard time leaving the cemetery as well: she had to be carried to the car. I could see E-Money's oldest daughter Shavonte trying to hold on and be strong. She had broken down the night of his death at the hospital and I know she was being strong and holding on with her auntie. Kenyette was in a world of silence. She wanted to cry but when she saw his children she held it in. She told me from the beginning that she would be there for me through it all and she truly had her mama's back.

My baby boy LaJuan was in a world of darkness. He had received the telephone call that E-Money was lying in the street all shot up. He was there with E-Money, his big brother when he took his last breath. I could see how hard it was for him but all I knew to do was pray. My Apostle told me to continue to pray and God will help us through this, "so stay prayerful," were her words.

My prayer will always be for God to bless each family member and to be their strength; let them know that you are the truth, the way and the life. (John 14: 6)
In Jesus name I pray.

Dinner At The Church

Dinner was prepared and everything was set up so beautiful and my church family has always believed in doing things in order. Pastor L'aShawn taught each of the staff when preparing food to always use that "extra touch." I knew my pastors had taken personal time out for the set-up along with my True Gospel family. I saw so many people that had come to my son's funeral enjoying the dinner afterward. They were talking, laughing, and eating and enjoying themselves.

They prepared my husband's and my plate, but I couldn't eat. I was hungry and the food looked so delicious but I couldn't eat a bite. My stomach had that feeling of weakness so I didn't eat. My husband ate somewhat and most of my grandchildren and family members ate and I was pleased to see them eat. My husband and I stayed just a short while, about 30 minutes to an hour. I heard different family members and friends comment on how good the food was.

I would like to thank my church again for all of their support. Keep trusting in the Lord and He will guide you and me all the way. Obedience is the key to the kingdom way of living.

Arriving Home After The Funeral

Coming home from the funeral was very difficult. Not only did I have to face the realization that I would not see my son anymore. I had to deal with my mother's illness not understanding what was really going on. My parents didn't attend the funeral because my mother was going through a stage of dementia and we as a family decided that we didn't want to let her know that her first grandchild had been murdered. Just telling her I believe would have killed her. My dad, her baby sister, Jean and my oldest, sister Yvonne, stayed at the house with her while we all attended the funeral. I got out of the limo and walked to my porch surprised to see so many people at my house so soon after I had just left the church. I wondered how so many people had gotten to the house before us. I knew it was going to be a long day. I asked God right then to give me strength. I really wanted some quiet time. When I approached the porch I discovered that many people brought food and a large number of people were people who just simply didn't like to attend funerals, came to the house for support. After I got home, my biggest concern was taking care of my mother, and trying to move my parents back to Detroit. She lives in Cassopolis, Michigan which is about three hours south of Detroit. My dad bought five acres of land there and built a five bedroom ranch home after his retirement in 1993 from General Motors.

My mom and my dad had been staying with me for about a week before my son's death. My mother was under doctor's care to determine her stage of dementia. She had gone to several doctors wanting a second opinion of her diagnosis. So my job before my son was murdered was to find a doctor here in Detroit that could answer that. We had been to three different kinds of doctors and we were waiting for the test results when my son E-Money was murdered.

The night my son was killed we tried to keep it from my daddy until the morning but he came out the guest room where he and my mom had been staying and wrapped me in his arms. He held me tight and told me that everything would be alright and that God don't make No mistakes. That felt good coming from my daddy, but more than ever, I really needed my mom. I felt so empty inside. My mother was my best friend. Before she got sick we prayed together every morning. We shared a love that only a mother and daughter could have. She was my everything and she still is. I want her back in full. I can see her, touch her, hold her, and kiss her that's all good. She can even talk to me, but she really does not understand what we are really talking about most of the time nor that I'm her daughter? I have a lot of questions. Will she ever get her mind back? Will she ever be able to hold a normal conversation? Will she ever know that her grandson has been murdered? I'm dealing with a lot right now and only God can help. I know that God doesn't put more on us than we can bear, so that's what I hold on to everyday. Trusting and knowing that God has my back. I must be strong remembering God is able. In every trial there is a revelation and I must believe that God is healing me, my mother, and each person that is hurting in this situation. We are going to have some ups and some downs in life but we must stand firm on God's word and we must learn how to trust him, not only when things are going our way but trust him in a situation like I'm in now. I needed to learn how to be consistent in praying morning, noon, and night again. I know that God created life and that the devil is here illegally. I know that the devil is trying to create a system here on earth for believers to become non-believers so I had to talk to the devil so he would flee. I must not allow him to come in. I must stay in prayer and I will come back with scripture from the bible. I will continue to repeat scripture after scripture and stand firm on Gods words.

I will continue to repeat:

No weapon form against me shall prosper

Proverbs 3: 5-6

5. Trust in the Lord with all your heart,
And lean not on your own understanding;
6. In all your ways acknowledge Him,
And He shall direct your paths.

Psalms 23:1-6

The Lord is my shepherd; "I shall not want. 2. He maketh me to lie down in green pastures: He leadth me beside the still waters. 3. He restoreth my soul: He leadeth me in the paths of righteousness for His name's sake. 4. Yea, though I walk through the valley of the shadow of death, I will fear no evil: for thou art with me; thy rod and thy staff they comfort me. 5. thou preparest a table before me in the presence of mine enemies: thou anointest my head with oil; my cup runneth over. 6. Surely goodness and mercy shall follow me all the days of my life: and I will dwell in the house of the Lord forever.

My prayer is for God to keep me and my family in His perfect peace. I will trust Him daily and take one day at a time. I know that this is a new beginning of a long time adjustment.

My First 30 Days of Grief

Not knowing what to do or which way to turn. I could feel the heaviness in my heart, as I lay still in my bed afraid to move, I began to have these sharp pains. I felt like I was having a heart attack. I couldn't think. It felt like a dream. Was my son really dead? Would I ever be the same? I needed some answers and there was nobody there to answer me. I knew how to pray and to call on God when in trouble. I knew that He was and is the only answer. I just couldn't get this. It's easy to praise God when things are going our way; how do you praise Him in a situation like this? I knew that God could do better with my life than I could. So this song came to my mind.

I Give Myself Away
Here I am, here I stand,
Lord my life is in your hands
Lord, I'm longing to see your desires revealed in me
I give myself away
Take my heart, take my life
As a living sacrifice
All my dreams all my plans
Lord I place them in your hands; I give myself away so you can use me.
My life is not my own, to you I belong.
I give myself; I give myself to you so you can use me.

I love that song and there is nobody that can sing it like my church choir Judea. I felt like my life was over. I didn't want to live. I wanted to give up. My mind was too troubled to think, I had no comfort. I just kept that song in my mind. I felt like I was losing self-control. I knew no words to speak. I felt there was no way out. I felt hopeless, helpless and out of touch. My heart was hurting and overwhelmed with pain and a heavy load. I knew that we all must face death someday and that God is in control. But I still felt empty, stressed out, like I had no family or friends, although my husband and all my family was right by my side and tried to comfort me. I didn't want to face reality. I didn't want to face my son or daughter. I didn't know how to explain their pain. I wanted to help them but at the time I couldn't help myself.

E-Money's children were my greatest worry. Again he had six. His daughter, Shavonte who's eighteen was a daddy's little girl, so I knew I had to be strong for her. I knew she was basically going through the same thing I was.

His son E-Money Jr. was sixteen years old and he's a very quiet person, he kept his feelings in. I knew he was hurting just as much as we were. Sydnee, the third child was distant and they shared a love unexplainable. Their love was special and I knew her mother, Tracy, would help Sydnee through this. The other three children really didn't understand death, but we explained to them that their daddy was up in heaven with Jesus. I did everything in my power to get my mind back connected with God. I was at the point where I hated the world. Why I hated the world, I don't know? What I know is that feeling was in me and I couldn't get rid of it. My personal relationship with Jesus Christ was all I had at that point. How do I get it back? Who was I becoming? Or what was I becoming? This wasn't me? I began to pray, God please remove these evil spirits from me.

Psalm 27:1
The Lord is my light and my salvation;
Whom shall I fear?
The Lord is the strength of my life?
Of whom shall I be afraid?
Proverbs 3:5-6:
5. Trust in the Lord with all your heart,
And lean not to your own understanding;
6. In all your ways acknowledge Him,
And He will direct your paths.

I really need direction. Can I truly be honest? I was mad. I was in desperate need for some serious help. I had gotten to the point where I wanted to kill. I knew nothing about how to kill but I felt if I could just have one minute with Boo, the person that murdered my son, and called me mom I would learn. I never wanted to kill anybody before this, but I felt like vengeance was mine. My thoughts were getting out of control. Any and everybody that knows me, always say I'm one of the sweetest people you could meet. Right about now I wasn't thinking about being sweet. All I wanted to do was have one minute alone with that boy, Boo, who as far as I was concerned, was a cold blooded murderer. Oh yes, I prayed to God every night for me to forgive him, because God is a forgiving God. I believe one day soon I will forgive him without a shadow of a doubt. But right now I'm not feeling it. **James 3:** Speaks about the untamable tongue: Just paraphrasing: The tongue is a fire. It's an unruly evil, full of deadly poison. With it we bless our God and Father, and with it we curse men. Out of the same mouth we proceed blessing, and cursing, that shall not be. I knew when that scripture came to mind I had to pull myself together. God knows what's going on inside of me so why should I lie? Right now I'm mad as hell with Boo. I began to reach out to God screaming from the top of my voice, asking Him to give me strength. I needed strength and I needed it now. I began to question God asking Him. Why? Why now? Why my son? Why did he have to go? He was just getting his life together. I know some people say you shouldn't question God. I never believed that because if God knows our thoughts, then He knows what we are thinking. And I was thinking just what I asked. I know there's nothing too hard for God, and I needed to get a better or clear understanding of what was going on. I couldn't think, I couldn't pray, I couldn't talk to God. It wasn't because I didn't want to because I did. But all I could do was think a lot of foolish thoughts. I knew certain scriptures from the bible like, **Roman 12:19** When God tells us that vengeance is His, and He will repay. And I knew the murderer would be arrested sooner or later. I knew I had to stand on God's word, but at that time I wanted vengeance to be mine. I read the Bible and I knew that this was a test and it was time to fight the devil with everything I knew. I still felt like I was losing my mind and I knew only God could help me. He never allows us to handle more than we can bear. Just as I was thinking these thoughts, my Bible was right in front of me. I picked it up and turned to **Psalm 91:1** He that dwelleth in the secret place of the most high shall abide under the shadow of the Almighty. The Holy Spirit, which lives inside of me, begin to take control of my body, after that, scriptures kept coming: **Psalms 121:2** My help cometh from the lord, which made heaven and earth. **Psalm 23:** The Lord is my shepherd, I shall not want. I knew God was working in me obedience, but to me I was fighting against it. The reason I say this is, all the good that God was showing me, and I kept going back. I had to shake that devil up and turn my thoughts around for good. I saw all my family and friends support but I didn't want it, all I wanted was to see, touch, and tell my son, "Mama is here." I was going into a pity stage. I began to wonder what happens to a person after death and where do they go? The Scripture, **St John 14:1-4**, came to my mind: 1. Let not your heart be troubled; you believe in God, believe also in me. 2. In My Father's house are many mansions, if it were not so, I would have told you. I go to prepare a place for you. 3. And if I go and prepare a place for you, I will come again, and receive you to Myself; that where I am, there ye may be also. 4. And where I go you know, and the way you know. This scripture answered my questions that I had just asked God: Where's my son? And what happens to a person after death? Now I knew God was here with me and I wasn't by myself in this. I began to feel the presence of the Holy Spirit all around me. I had a beautiful feeling in my body, mind and soul. The feeling was unexplainable, but I felt a peace and I knew God had heard my cry. I immediately stopped feeling like the whole world was against me, and begin to trust in God. **Philippians 4:13** read; "I can do all things through Christ which strengtheneth me."

Dear God, You are showing and teaching me a lot. I will continue to trust and serve you all the days of my life. I thank and praise your Holy name. This is where I want to stay in your presence.

Giving In To Satan

Life was just another day to me. I was trying to learn how to take one day at a time. When my husband and I came home from the funeral, there were a lot of friends and relatives still hanging around. Kenyette, my daughter lived two doors down from me on the right and my son LaJuan lived two doors down on the left. Kenyette had her friends and a crowd outside of her house. Looking down the street to my left was LaJuan with his friends and a crowd. Well I'm the president of our block club and we never had that much excitement on our block before. Most of the neighbors are in their 50's and well settled. Some of them were at my house waiting for me to come in. When I entered the house anybody and everybody was there waiting to cheer me up. I began to get really depressed. I had a lot of cousins here from out of town that I use to party with back in the day over 20 years ago. They knew that I didn't allow drinking in my house, so most of them drank on the porch or went down to my daughter or son's house which they had no problem with the drinking.

While my husband, Leon was socializing with our family and friends, I eased away and went upstairs to lie down. After being upstairs for minutes by myself, I just sat there crying and wondering what was I going to do with my life? How can I get through this? Just as I saw myself heading into a stage of depression, two of my family members came upstairs to check on me. They were older than I and I hadn't seen them in a long time. They tried to cheer me up by talking about the worldly things we did years ago. I laughed with them and began to feel a little better. One of them said, "Girl I know you don't allow drinking alcohol in your house, but Jesus turned water into wine. I got a case of this white and red wine in my car, you need to take a drink to ease your pain, girl."

I agreed and that one time turned into a 30 to 40 day journey. I didn't tell my husband or those family members that introduced the wine to me in the first place. I went from expensive wine, to Miller High Life beer, from one - 12 ounce to two 12 ounces. I started sneaking beer in the house drinking in the bathroom. I had to go across eight mile to buy my beer because I didn't want anybody to know I was drinking. After two weeks went by and I saw I couldn't stop I told my husband that I picked up a drinking habit. He knew that I had drunk beer and coolers before so he didn't think anything was wrong with me having a little drink here and there. He didn't give me a chance to tell him the real deal. He was just going on my pass and knew that I never would finish a whole beer when I did drink.

Little did he know he was in for a surprise of his life. Well the first thirty days of my son's death I didn't go back to work. I own my own clothing store in the neighborhood and most of the neighbors knew my son was murdered so I stayed closed. Leon took two weeks off so I had some comfort. My pastors were calling and visiting and no one had a clue. I needed help but who could I tell. Satan had crept in and I knew I had to get rid of that no good devil. My question was "How?" Who can help me? I'm too embarrassed to tell my pastors. I had heard a voice whisper, "Tell me, tell me." I knew then where my help would come from. I begin to pray. I thought since I heard from God and I prayed that in the morning, once I got up, my problem from drinking would be over.

Leon was up and he was returning back to work. Oh boy, it was just me and the bottle. I couldn't wait some days for him to hurry up and leave so I could go to the store and buy me two 12 ounce Miller beers. Well I didn't want to wait any more so I bought me a twelve pack of Millers and a six pack of wine coolers. I didn't want to get fat from drinking so much beer so I decided to drink beer one day and coolers the next. It didn't take my husband long to notice something wasn't right with me. I had to tell him what was going on and how long it had been going on. He told me that E-Money was so proud of me for not drinking, smoking and living a wild life so why am I allowing the devil to take control of me. I tried again to get myself together, that was week three after E-Money's death. I stopped for two days and that was it. I kept it a secret again from my husband. I wanted to stop but I couldn't sleep at night. The beer and cooler would help me sleep. I have a prayer partner that I had been praying with for over three years daily at six o'clock every morning three days a week. I had been praying with her and I never told her. As I started to pray with her this particular morning out of nowhere came, "And God please help me to stop drinking!" When I finished it was her turn to pray. We normally pray fifteen to twenty minutes each. This morning she prayed about an hour and one thing I remember her saying, "is the next time Evelyn picks up a bottle to drink make her sick, remove that spirit of drinking beer away from her." That prayer stayed in my head all day and I was kind of mad. Why is she praying for me to get sick if I drink some beer again? Who does she think she is? Ain't nobody perfect. Here I go again with that ain't nobody perfect gesture.

When it was time for me to go to bed, I got my beer from my closet and went into the bathroom. I had to drink the beer fast that time because I had took my bath earlier and I couldn't stay in the bathroom to long without Leon suspecting something. I was actually sick to my stomach. The beer began to come back up. Leon asked what was wrong and told me to open the door. When I did there sat the beer bottle which was the evidence to what was wrong! He said I had to fight the devil and take full control back over my life. It was at that moment I knew I was really going to start fighting back. I had a habit and I needed help. That was the fourth week after E-Money death. It was just about time for me to start preparing myself to get back to work. What am I going to do? Prayer had been taking care of me so far so let me go back to prayer.

Ilamani was born October 1, 1974. This picture was taken December 1, 1974 Mother and Son

I Began To Pray

God Took Me

To The Day

Of

My Son's Birth

E-Money's Birth

October 1, 1974 marked the happiest day of my life; the birth of my first born child at the age of 20. He was truly a gift from God. Not being a God fearing mother, at the time of my son's birth, raised questions in my mind. It was on that day, while holding my son in my arms, I knew God was real. I never knew how having a baby could change a life. Having E-Money changed my life for the better. He immediately changed my life and my way of thinking. After having him I immediately wanted to learn everything I could about that creator people call God. Don't get me wrong, I knew of Him, my mom and dad raised me up in the church and I was baptized at the age of twelve. I went to Sunday school and sung in the choir every Sunday, but I wasn't taught to be a God fearing child or woman, although I was taught the Ten Commandments at the church I attended.

They put the commandments in their own words, not teaching us from the bible or instructing us to read the bible for ourselves. I never knew where to find the Ten Commandments or anything else in the bible. We didn't have the teachings back then like they have today, or may I say, most pastors didn't share what books they were studying from and got their information. I knew nothing about a simple English Bible, or a step by step how to study the bible book. All I knew was the King James Version and back then it was so hard to understand, so I just learned what I was taught in church, on TV, and at home. I was mainly taught that no one was perfect, and we all have sinned and come short of God's glory. With all that programmed in my mind, when I did do something that wasn't right, it really wasn't a big deal to me, because I lived by the words I was taught. No one is perfect and we all have sinned. The church I attended focused on teaching no sex before you were grown or married and at that time you were grown at eighteen. By me being only 12 years old, sex never even crossed my mind. So I waited until I was out of high school and out of my Parents house before I had a relationship. I'm not blaming the church that I attended for my actions or choices that I made; I just think they should have been straight forward instead of beating around the bush. I truly believe if I would have been taught right, I would have been one out of a thousand that would have waited until marriage. I'm not regretting the birth of my son, as I said earlier, that was the happiest day of my life. I'm just saying, pastors are the key to a person learning the truth and teaching the truth about the Bible, so

Sunday school teachers and Bible study teachers, or any other leader shouldn't sugar coat the word, they should be bold and tell it like it is.

When E-Money was born

The day I went into labor it was my mom's birthday; she was having a small get together at the house that day and I was helping with the house cleaning and getting everything in order for her birthday celebration. I was 9 months and expecting to have my baby any day. My mother really wanted the baby to be born on her birthday, mainly because that would be her first grandchild.

Around 7:00 p.m. my mother's friends started to arrive. I greeted most of her guest, which was family and friends but after that I stayed in my room, because I was a little tired from cleaning the house earlier that day. While in my bedroom lying down resting, mild pains began to come. The pain got sharper and sharper so about two hours into her party, I announced that I was experiencing mild labor pains and I believed it was time for the baby to come. It was like a television comedy, everybody in the house started screaming and running around the house as if they had never been around a person going into labor. They all scared the heck out of me. Then my mother took charge and said, "calm down, let's get her to the hospital." I said, "Wait, can I take a shower?" My mother said, "You just took a shower earlier." I felt like another shower was needed. After I took my shower and came out ready to go to the hospital, I saw all the neighbors. My mother and family members had called the whole block down to go to the hospital with us.

E-Money at six weeks with his uncle Luther

[53]

At The Hospital

At the hospital there were about 25 to 30 people, all family and friends. E-Money's birth was like a little king being born. I was happy and at the same time I was scared. I really didn't know anything about having a baby. I was waiting for my mother to tell me the big secret that all women should know when having a baby. Little did I know there was no big secret. Having a baby was as real as real could get. Listen to this, I truly thought that I was carrying water and food in my stomach and when my nine months was up and it was time for me to have my baby, that my mother and doctor would tell me the big secret, just like Christmas and Santa. How could I be so wrong? I remember asking questions at the age of twelve years old about having babies and wearing makeup and all that girly girl stuff. I was told by my parents and other adults to wait until you get grown, or go somewhere and play, leave me alone. They would never give me a straight answer, so throughout my childhood life all I knew was the basics of a boy and girl.

In the beginning of high school I took a class called personal relations, which was supposed to teach us about relationships. All we learned was how to use different birth controls and how to keep our bodies clean. We basically learned personal hygiene. Not once from home, school or church was I ever taught the real deal behind having sex. My girlfriends and I would make up stories about having a boyfriend and getting married and having babies, not knowing anything about being a mother, we were just having fun talking that girly girl talk in our teenage years. I was in for the surprise of my life.

The Labor Pains Begin

At first everybody in my hospital room was laughing and having a good time but before long the labor pains began to come. I was waiting for my mother to tell me the big secret about having a baby then the pain got deeper and deeper. I began to feel pressure and the pain got deeper. The doctor and nurse kept coming in checking on me then a strange look came over my mother's face and she began to pray. Now my mother prayed all the time, I could hear her praying early in the morning and late at night, but why was she praying for me right then? Little did I know, I was about to experience the greatest experience women living could ever experience. Just then, in came two or three doctors and nurses coming into the room and they asked everybody to leave.

"Wait a minute," I said, what's going on? Before they could answer another deep pain came on, this pain was different from the other pain I was having just minutes before. It felt like my whole insides was pushing itself out; not understanding that it was time for the baby to come, I begin to scream, "help me mother! This pain is too much for me." My mother looked at me with tears in her eyes saying, "Baby it's going to be alright." Then she asked the doctor to put me to sleep. I shouted out, "NO, NO, I don't want to go to sleep! I want to see the birth of my child!" The doctors told me to calm down, and that he would give me something to ease my pain. My mother stayed there with me holding my hand and praying. I remember hearing her say God you never give us more than we can bear, so please let my baby's pain be light. I also heard her pray for me not to stay in labor long. When the doctor examined me, it was about 11:30 p.m. He told my mother that it was going to be a long night so they could leave and come back in the morning. My mother told him she would stay a little longer to keep an eye on me and he agreed and left the room. When my family and friends came back in the room to say their goodbyes it was about 11:59 p.m. The reason I knew what time it was is because my mother kept looking at the clock. She wanted her first grandchild to be born on her birthday. Then at 12:01 a.m. my mother laughed and said, "Maybe the next one." As everybody was ready to leave, I began to cough and hiccup, and I couldn't stop so my mother called the nurse back in the room. When she examined me she said, "Oh God, her water has broken, there is the baby's head. She then asked everybody to leave and she called the doctor. I don't remember what happened after that. I think I fainted or something, so I lost the last ten minutes of what was going on. When I gained consciousness, I was on the operating table, and the doctor, nurse and my mother was saying, "Push... the baby is here and ready to come out." I knew I had to be strong this time so I could really see what was happening so I began to push. Then E-Money came out. It was a miracle happening right before my face. A long beautiful baby boy, he came out kicking and crying. I was told that most babies had to get spanked by the doctor when they first come out to indicate that they are alive, but in E-Money's case he came out kicking and crying. I was so happy and proud. I felt like a million dollars, so you know what I mean. I heard my mother often sing and this song came to my mind: I'm blessed, I'm truly blessed.

Even then I thought about his first day of school. All kinds of thoughts started coming to mind. My son wasn't even a day old yet, and I had big questions about, how I was going to take good care of my baby without a daddy. I knew that whatever it took to be a good mother to my son I would learn.

My whole life changed. E-Money is the reason I know and love God the way that I do. When he came into this world and into my life I saw the light. It was then I wanted to be a true child of God. So I picked up my Bible and begin reading Genesis. In the beginning God created the heaven and the earth. He was the beginning of my salvation.

The meaning of salvation is saved from danger. E-Money, in some sense, rescued me. He saved my life from the sinful ways. All I wanted to do when he was born was to do everything right. As I sit back remembering the first day that he came home from the hospital, and all the gifts my sister Syria had bought. I could truly say E-Money lived like a king his first three years. Knowing that he wasn't a real king, or nowhere compares to my true king Jesus. He was a little king in my eyes. My brothers and sisters played a big part in helping me to raise him. He had everything as a child; most of all he had a lot of love. During this time I got a job at a restaurant named Jack-In-the-Box. My mother, father, brothers and sister would babysit E-Money while I worked. My mother and father both worked. My dad worked at General Motors and my mother worked at Lear's Jet. E-Money was the first grandchild and he had so much love. E-Money was spoiled by his uncles and his aunts. He was taught not to steal, kill, or sell drugs at an early age.

About

Me

And

My

Family

I Met And Married The Love Of My Life Leon

I lived with my mom and dad off and on after E-Money's birth for about two to three years. During my stay and moving back and forth I had a beautiful baby girl, I named her Kenyette. Her name came from a favorite cousin named Kenneth, who had committed suicide during my pregnancy. I loved and missed him so much. I thought it would be a good idea to name her after him. When Kenyette was born, E-Money was going on age two. When he saw Kenyette from day one he took care of her. He tried to feed her chicken, chips everything he had he wanted her to have also. He didn't understand that she was a baby and she couldn't have the same things he had. When they were old enough to play together they shared their toys and candy. E-Money and Kenyette were more than brother and sister they became best friends.

I had been dating Leon off and on for over three years. He asked me to marry him, we married and he adopted E-Money as his son. After a few years we had enough money saved up to buy a house. We moved in the house where we are still living today, where our third child LaJuan was born just months before we moved into our new home. Again E-Money loved his little brother LaJuan just as much as he loved Kenyette when she was a baby. They both together took good care of their little brother. E-Money took care of the both of them until his death. God has been in our life and we as a family love God. We grieve together knowing that God will help each of us get through this. We must trust Him and have the faith of a mustard seed.

E-Money Growing up in the Neighborhood

When E-Money was twelve he had asked if he could get a paper route. We found out more about it and he became the paperboy for our street and the next street over. That was his first job besides making money shoveling snow or cutting grass. After he got the job he bought himself a penny bank and started saving money. He wanted a mini bike but his dad and I told him that a mini bike was too dangerous, but when he got old enough and save his money he could buy one. So from the age of twelve to about fourteen he kept his paper route. After a few years he had a lot of streets added to his route and his sister was working right beside him. He had stopped thinking about a mini bike and he was now saving money for a car. He never saved more than a hundred dollars, because every time a new style of shoes came out at Foot Locker he wanted them. He spent most of his money on shoes. All we had to buy were his clothes and his food. He kept his bedroom nice and neat and put his clothes in the cleaners when needed. He learned that from his daddy and his uncles.

Later E-Money applied for a job at Mc Donald's and got the job. At that time he had just graduated from junior high. This was during his first semester in high school. All E-Money's friends called him money because he always had money. He started working at the age of twelve, and now he was working at McDonald's and was a paperboy. He never had an attitude for people to give him anything, he believed in working for it. Now with me it was different. He thought when he asked mom or dad for something we just had to give it to him. He didn't ask us for too much growing up as a child because we always kept the necessities. From time to time in his older years, he came to me as if I were a bank. As a mother sometimes I allowed him to use me as his bank and to be honest his daddy Leon did also. We knew when to and when not to be his personal bank.

What Happened in High School

After a while E-Money gave up the job as a paperboy. He was still into buying shoes and saving his money. Once he bought himself a pair of money green Gucci shoes. He smiled for days when he wore those shoes. During high school one of his neighborhood friends saw him in the hall while going to class and asked him to come into the bathroom for a minute because he had something to show him. E-Money went in the bathroom with his friend and his friend showed E-Money a gun. His friend had taken the gun out his house without permission. The gun belonged to his friend's father. The boy asked E-Money if he could wear his Gucci shoes and he could carry the gun until school got out. E-Money agreed. What a big mistake, E-Money saw now how easy trouble was to get into. The boy that gave him the gun went straight to class. E-Money however, saw some of his other friends on his way to class, and he wanted to show off the gun, right in the hallway. He lifted up his pant leg where he had put the gun and all the boys gathered around him. The security guard saw the crowd and asked why weren't they in class. He then noticed E-Money pulling his pant leg down as well as the noticeable bulge in his pant leg. So he told the other boys to go to class and he took E-Money to the office. While inside the office he told E-Money to take the drugs from his pant legs, E-Money told him that he didn't have any drugs. The security guard then called the principle but still they didn't believe that E-Money was free of drugs. When E-Money said it was a gun and not drugs, the police was called and E-Money was suspended from all Detroit Public Schools. He had to go to a juvenile court, where they saw that he was a good boy that made a bad decision. He was placed on probation for two years. The judge stated that if he stayed out of trouble the gun charge would be removed from his record. After that we enrolled E-Money into a high school outside of Detroit. For two years after that E-Money did not get into any trouble and the gun case was removed from his record.

Our Neighborhood Was Getting Out Of Order

Watching the kids grow-up from children to teenagers was a good feeling, but murders were happening in our neighborhood on a continuous basis. When E-Money was about sixteen years old a girl that was in his classroom was murdered; she was found shot to death in her car. They later found out that she was murdered by a young man she was dating who happened to be much older than her. In that same year a boy that went to his school was shot to death at the bus stop. They never knew who or why he was murdered. Every summer at least two or three neighborhood kids were getting killed. One summer a boy that lived on my street was killed in a car accident, along with a young girl who died too, his cousin was driving the car. It was later told that they were drinking and driving. His cousin lived but was charged with driving drunk under the influence of alcohol. He served three years in jail because he was driving drunk and two people died in the accident. After he did his three years and was released from jail, he wasn't home a year before he was shot to death while sleeping over a girlfriend's house who had a jealous ex- boyfriend. He was a good boy who had bad luck in his life. I still pray for his family. I remember hearing E-Money talk about another accident when some of his friends were driving home from a party, when a car jumped from one lane into their lane hitting their car and one of the passengers was thrown through the window. While waiting on the ambulance to come to take the boy to the hospital, would you believe that another car came by and hit and killed him. How bad can this world be? Death was all around the neighborhood. I read in the paper about somebody kicking the door in on a man two blocks over and he was robbed and shot to death. Dying, killing, and murder was all over the neighborhood. If you didn't know the person that was killed or murdered, you knew somebody in their family. That's just how close death was to us in the neighborhood. Not only was killing happening in my neighborhood, it was happening on the northside, eastside, westside, southside, downtown, uptown even in the suburbs.

My children and I went to church almost every Sunday. I had begun to be afraid of my own neighborhood but I never let my children know. My husband and I talked about moving a lot, but because we had paid cash for our home and had spent so much money into it we kept coming back to an agreement to stay. I prayed to God to keep my children from all hurt, harm, and danger and all the madness in this world. I often talked to my children about their friends, drinking, driving, and drugs and to always try to make the right decision. I never dreamed that something like murder would happen to one of my own. I just wanted them to understand how easy it was to lose your life. I raised them in church because I wanted them to learn everything they could about living a Godly life. I knew that somewhere in the Bible it spoke about if you raise your child up Godly, they may stray away but they will come back to Christ. E-Money may have backslidden at times in his life, but there is one thing I can say; he had the opportunity to have a relationship with our Father, Lord Jesus. I learned early in life how to pray for our neighborhoods and family. I believe that is an important part for parents to play in their children's life while growing up.

Coming home from church one Sunday we stopped at the gas station to get them some snacks, they were told by one of their friends that a boy named Rico that they had known had gone to sleep while driving home from the club. He had driven his car head on into an eighteen wheeler truck and died in the accident. Later that week my best girlfriend's daughter and grandson died in a house fire. People were dying all around us. My cousin was killed by a man while arguing over a girl. This was my cousin's brother that killed himself one year later on the same date because he didn't want to live any more without his brother.

E-Money had a longtime friend who moved out of town because of all the violence in the neighborhood. He was also a good boy and he left to start a new life. He loved to ride mini bikes and motor bikes. He died later on his motor bike. E-Money would talk to me constantly about how fake most of the guys are in the streets and that he only hung out with them because somebody knows what happened to his cousin "Double O" (Tezo) who had been murdered nine years earlier than E-Money and the case was never solved. E-Money never ever would have become friends with Boo or any of the guys around the corner. He started off hanging with Boo's brother, T-bone, because the rumor was T-bone knew who murdered "Double O." E-Money said he wanted to get to the bottom of his cousin's death. He believed that the police closed the case because it was drug related. So, E-Money started his own investigation.

Drug dealers were getting killed left and right in our neighborhood. If one person made more money than the other or if you sold to their customers you could get "iced" (killed). My nephew, Double O, was murdered in his van and they never found out why he was murdered or who murdered him. Two weeks before Double O was shot and murdered one of his friends was shot and robbed. They (police) never knew who did it at least they never said. E-Money and LaJuan was close to their cousin but they didn't hang with the crowd that he hung with, so when Double O was murdered he was with that crowd not with his cousins. People in the neighborhood who knew him told his mother, my sister Syria, that T-Bone and Boo knew exactly who murdered him. We told E-Money to let the police handle it but he loved his cousin and he wanted to find out who killed him. He would come home at night and tell us that T-Bone and Boo told a different story about what happened every time they told the story. E-Money was waiting for them to slip up. They never did the first year, so E-Money stopped hanging with them. Two years later T-Bone and Boo came over on to our block and started coming over every day. They started calling me mom and E-Money bro, so we claimed them as family. That led my son to his death. How could we have trusted a cold blooded murderer? How could you murder a friend? Why did the murderer call me mom? I will always wonder what really happened the night my son was murdered. Over 20 murders had happened in my neighborhood. I personally knew most of the victims.

Watching the news on TV had gotten to the point that all you would hear about is murder. It is sad to see brothers killing brothers, sisters killing sisters, friends killing friends, loved ones killing loved ones. Does this generation realize that it's hard enough to bury a love one that dies of natural causes then you have to turn around and bury someone who has been murdered? What is this world coming to? E-Money's death was nine years after his cousin's Double O's death, and this time somebody spoke up. Did they speak up enough? No, because if they would have the murderer would have been charged with 1st degree murder instead of 2nd degree. Did they see what happened and just let it happen? Why didn't they just tell the whole truth? Why did the murderer, kill my son?

Thank you for speaking up. E-Money is buried next to his cousin "Double O." Rest In Peace My Sons.

E-Money, Darzell

Double O with his daughter

LaJuan & Double O

Jasmone and her mom Jayne

More Talk About E-Money Before High School

I spoke against selling drugs, stealing, disrespecting your elders all my life to my children. That wasn't an issue for my children. E-Money tried to sell weed once in his earlier adulthood, but once Leon and I found out, he gave it up. We explained to him about the trouble that comes with selling drugs. E-Money listened and he never tried again. Selling drugs was the biggest problem we had in our neighborhood. Young boys that I knew as kids are now standing on the corners and have become drug dealers. They never had over $100.00 in their pockets; they just wanted to be in the in crowd. How sad and where were their parents? I raised E-Money only on what I knew. I taught him love and respect, and he grew up as a very respectable young man, I must say. I didn't see it at first how respectable my son was because I had to spank him often for talking under his breath to me. But everywhere I went people would tell me how respectable my son was. While E-Money was growing up I didn't allow him to go off the block until he was sixteen years old. All E-Money's friends had to come to his house, unless I took him over to his best friends' house, Juan Eades., or Marcelles Bell. I would drop him off and pick him up until I got to know that they was truly good boys, good boys they are even after his death. E-Money went to private school for two years until I got laid off from General Motors. My money got short so I enrolled him in a Detroit Public School. I went to school with him every day. I did volunteer work for the school and worked in the lunch room. The reason I was so protective during that time, young boys were shooting boys just because of the clothes they wore. I had to do what I felt was necessary for my kids to be protected. E-Money hated that and always mumbled under his breath behind my back. I would hear him but acted as if I didn't. My lifetime prayer to God has always been for God to protect and keep my children in His care. E-Money knew my daily prayer and he would always say God has got his back through my prayers. I would laugh and say through yours also.

E-Money's First Time off the Block

When E-Money turned sixteen his daddy Leon insisted that I let E-Money go around the corner and off the block. I knew it was time for me to let him go places without me dropping him off and picking him up, but that was a big mistake. After six months I noticed trouble had begun. He started breaking his curfew and different girls started calling the house. He wanted to hang around the block every day. Well after talking to him and getting a better understanding about his curfew, things begin to work out fine. He started dating a girl around the block that was a couple of years older than him who had a baby boy already. I met her a few times and she was a nice young girl. So I was fine with that.

About one year into their relationship to my surprise E-Money was on his way to becoming a father. Not knowing what to do or say, because he was still in school and he knew nothing about being a father. I decided to help out with whatever. He had a job at Mc Donald's and he was a paper boy. That was not the problem. The problem was his age and he was still in school. Like I said earlier, the girl was older and experienced; she had a baby already. I was scared and felt responsible. The girl was very nice and sweet. I use to cook breakfast for my son and family: bacon, eggs, grits and toast but that young lady began to bring him breakfast almost every morning. She cooked steak, potatoes, hash browns, eggs and even brought juice. When she didn't come around with his breakfast he would leave and go to her house to eat. I think I got a little jealous because my son loved my cooking but now he didn't give it the time of day. I had never cooked steak for breakfast.

Time went on in their relationship and I agreed to help them raise my grandchild to be. Little did I know that would end up being a lifetime promise that I kept and trust me I'm still keeping it right to this day. She was a pretty baby and I kept her most of the time, all she wanted was me. She wanted me to take her everywhere I went. After her birth, E-Money and Wynnie the girl around the block, moved into an apartment together. Time went on and they birthed a beautiful baby boy Ilamani, Jr. They saw something was missing so later on in life they ran off to Ohio and got married. After all they went through to get together they separated and were divorced after being together for over ten years. I never knew the real reason why they separated, but I do know he stayed in contact with his children until his death. They loved him dearly and he loved them. He always picked them up. They never missed a family reunion or a holiday dinner. He had much love for his kids and made sure that I did to. Wynnie later met and married a nice young man name Jocquez that E-Money met and they became friends. That made it easy for the children to have both a good father and a good stepfather in their life.

Later, E-Money had three other children: Sydnee, Azariah, and Emmanuel and right before his death he had a three week old baby boy, Kameron, and was engaged to the love of his life, a wonderful young lady name China. All his children know and love one another. E-Money you will always be remembered by the love you had and shared with others.

I would like to say to his children, whatever you do in life keep it real, because your daddy was a real man. He told people the truth and didn't sugar coat it. If you wanted to know the real deal about how you looked or something as simple as a hair style, he would tell you the real. It was so easy to love him.

To You My Son: You spoke the words of truth to your crowd. Mama love and miss you, but God showed me that you are in His care. So I'm ending this segment as your real best friend mom. See you on the other side baby.

A Word from E-Money to His love Ones

Why is everybody crying? Because you think you won't see me anymore. I'm sorry but you know it's not that easy to get rid of me. Our Heavenly Father has rescued me, and set my mind, body, and soul free.

I tossed and turned and I really wasn't ready to go, and that you all know. But I learned to listen; as you all know when God called I had no choice. I must go with His flow.

I know I'm missed, and so are you. Here's a great big kiss from me to you.

I'm asking a big favor as I normally do, from you, you and especially you. Do the one thing that God ask of us, love your neighbor as He loves us. You all know I follow that one, because of the love my mom gave and shared with everyone she came in contact with. Love is something you don't want to miss.

Most people are saying I was shot by my friend. He didn't have a clue of love from the beginning or end.

He says he's sorry and made a mistake. Our God forgave him for goodness sake. God knows whose real and God knows who is fake, my so call friend made a big mistake.

He shot to kill, is that how real friends feel. I lay here and wonder from a heavenly hill.

He took my life and he didn't even think twice. He knew my biggest plan this year was to make China, my wife.

I see her crying each and every night; baby I love you and I will always be holding you tight.

Go on with your life, and raise our son, teach him to love from his heart and let him know that daddy was with him from the start.

Teach him how to be a God fearing man, learning and loving God's master plan.

Tell our other three boys, that I helped you to raise, I feel their love and I love them too, and remember what I always told them, be good in school and follow your rules and obey their mother, most of all love one another, and help you to take care of their little brother. I hear Shavonte crying right now, so I got to go, I love you China and God loves you more.

To you Shavonte, my oldest girl, I hear you crying morning, noon and late at night, always remember daddy holding you tight. Trust in God and do what's right. God loves you so much and he'll keep you in his prefect sight. Go to church and study God's Word. Take care of your brothers and sisters and help them in life. Teach them as daddy taught you and I know they will grow up as sweet, kind, loving and as beautiful as you.

I know you don't really understand death too clear or why I had to die this year. One thing I want you to know is have no fear, God has me in His perfect care and I'll always be near. So my beautiful daughter who I love so dear, try not to worry or have no fear, just remember I'm always near.

I have four other children who I just have to mention. I'm watching over them with my full attention. Name by name and one by one, my love for them all will never be erased.

To you EJ, my oldest son, so handsome and tall, stay in school and get that scholarship for basketball. You are my big man with the master plan, and you know right from wrong, so I'm trusting that you stay real strong. Take care of the family and pull them through. My last words are Daddy really love you.

Sydnee, Sydnee my third sweet child, whose mother allowed you in my life off and on for a little while. When you came to visit I could see, all the love you had inside for me, and that big beautiful smile I love to see. Daddy's gone to a better place, remember that daddy love you and that could never be erased or replaced. So be the best that you can be in everything you do. Daddy is pushing you forward and I will always be with you.

To Azariah and Emmanuel, this is very hard you see, those two little ones really love me. I love them too, and that they know. Listen up my little babies who I left behind, God took me up to heaven to renew my mind. I enjoyed every minute I spent with you, taking the both of you to the store, parks, driving you around in my truck and listening to all the questions you would ask and especially all the times you both said I love you daddy and all the hugs and kisses. Baby girl and baby boy, you both remain in my heart and you both are truly missed. Be good in life and take care of each other. My biggest command is obey your mother and love one another.

What's up Little Chris, my number one homie. You were my first nephew and only nephew for nine years. You called me uncle, but I felt like your dad. I enjoyed watching you grow up to a fine young man. I still remember like yesterday, giving you the many pony rides on my back and neck. I know how strong your love is for me, just remember little homie, God set me free and now I'm hanging in heaven. Isn't that where I should be? So listen up and get this straight, don't be a follower and hang out late. Be a leader and do what's right and read your Bible morning, noon and night. I want you to always remember I love you, but guess what, God loves you more and He is always watching over you. Here's something I want you to do, always respect your mother and all the grown-ups around you. Talk to people with full respect, God is watching you. I know you will do your best because you always have listened to me, so this is your test. Peace and much love my little homie.

To my nephew Little Leshard who is three years old, and my baby niece Ren-Ren, who I love so dear. I know you are too small and don't understand what happened to me this year. Every time I saw the two of you we played hide and seek or peek-a-boo. So I guess I can say I'm out of town. I shared two years and more with the both of you. How happy you made me when we played peek-a-boo. I'm sorry I left so soon in your life. Remember to be good and remember I love the both of you. Look to the sky and be your best. Uncle Money is going now to rest.

Love You Sis

I'm still your big bro. So let's get something straight. I know you love and miss me, and I love and miss you too. Now we always knew this day would come. We never knew when and we never knew how, but we knew that God's timing is not our timing. I told you I was scared and you said you were too. Now I'm all grown up and so are you. I want you to listen to me real hard: my love for you will never part. This is a brand new world for me, and I'm doing fine, I will never let you or our family out of my mind. I know you are sad and I feel your pain. Stop crying so much, our love still remains. It had to happen and that you know. I wasn't really ready and that you know. I know you are sad and even mad. I see now God is the best thing I ever had. I want you to know, God's ways aren't our ways and His thinking is not like ours either, so He picked me out, because my heart was as a good achiever. Get serious about God and study His Word. God is the best thing that could have ever happened to me. The love I have for everybody was a gift from God and it was very strong. God watched me grow and changed my life. He knew all my rights and wrongs. I saw you get married and how happy you could be. Enjoy your husband and your family. Do what God say's to do in His Word. Raise your children and teach them what's right and God will continue to watch over you all morning, noon, and every night. **Love your big Bro forever and a day.**

E-Money age seven and Kenyette age six

E-Money age three Kenyette age two

Love You Bro

Hey little Bro, Where can I begin? You are more than my brother you are my best friend. I see you crying and I am too. As time goes by we will make it through. I know it was hard holding my hand and watching me fight while taking my last breath. Thank God that you were there and remember God knows best. I know you love me and I love you too. God called and I had to go, I tried not to answer, but God showed me a gleam of how my new life would be. Love, peace, joy, and happiness were all I could see. I had to answer so my soul could be free. We will see each other again my lifetime brother and my true best friend. Do what is right, you know what I mean. Watch over our family and help with the dream. We will all meet in heaven on the same team. I want you to be happy and don't be sad. I thank God for letting you be there with me that night so my little brother be glad and not sad. It was time for me to leave my earthly crew. I know it's hard for you to understand, but get in Church and follow God's commands. He will guide you through. So do me a favor I just had to ask, be the best you can be, and do the best you can do, and our heavenly Father will guide you through. Tell Amber that I love her and I miss her too. I'm sorry I will miss the wedding but I'll be there in spirit. I know you will be a good husband and she will be a good wife. So trust in God and remember everything we ever talked about. Remember who to trust. Let go of everybody and start new. Love, peace and joy will follow you. Keep in touch with our uncles and listen to dad and do what he says, he's always right. God is watching over you now and forever.

Love your big bro, Money.

[73]

E-Money at age 13 with his little brother Juan age 4

To You China My True Love

Hey Baby, Sorry I had to go so soon, I know we had just got our relationship on the right track. I asked you to marry me and to become my wife. I thank you for accepting and didn't think twice. My love for you was strong and clear; sorry I had to leave you alone this year. I know it's hard on you with our son and all, but baby I had to go when our Heavenly Father called. I wanted to stay, but I had to answer. I do know I'll see you again someday. Stay strong and keep your head up high, and remember that God is in full control of our lives. Raise all four boys in church as we were about to start and teach them to love each other and God with all their heart. The love we shared together will always be treasured. As time go on, you will see life goes on. I know you will always remember the love we shared, so my sweet little China who I love so dear, cheer up and raise the boys Kameron, Cortez, Khalil, and Caron. Let them know I will always love them and to be good in school, the sky is the limit.

Love Ilamani (E-Money)

To Mom and Dad

Mama I see you crying and hurting so much inside. Remember what you said to me all my life. God is perfect in all His ways and He never makes a mistake. You also told me that God might not come when we want Him but He's always on time. So I say to you trust in God as you have always told me. I see Daddy trying to help you through. Daddy has always pulled the family through every time we needed him, so mama, let daddy help you, and God will do the rest. I love you and stay strong in the Lord. Hey daddy you are a strong man and a good father. I thank you and love you too. Keep holding mama and do what you do. I know what you told me, just as mom did; I wish I would have listened like I have always said when you would get me out of something. I know if you could have saved me, you would have. You always kept me out of trouble. Now I see, God allowed things to happen this way. I just want you, mama and the family to know God allowed me to see a gleam and said it is time to go. I know I will see you and mama again someday. But until then keep it real like you always have.

Love your son Ilamani (E-Money)

Ilamani with his arms up saying show me some love!

E-Money, Kenyette, Gerald and Juan

In God's Care

To My Aunts and Uncles

Uncle Luke and Uncle Joe, I know you are mad and you had my back. All I can say is I love you and I thank you both for being a big part of my life. Uncle Mike, Uncle Tootie, and Uncle Todd I love and miss you too; take good care of each other and see you on the other side. Uncle Edward, Uncle Mike Money, Uncle Tony, Uncle James, Uncle John, and Uncle Bernard, thanks for your love and support. Uncle Earl, Uncle Red, Uncle Larry, thanks for your love and support. Tell Aunt Althea, Aunt Neice, and Auntie Sara, I know it was hard for them but thanks for coming to my home going. Let them know that I love and miss them so.

To Aunt Louise, I feel your pain.
It's all right my love for you still remain.
To Auntie Syria, so strong and cool,
my love for you will never be removed.
Aunt Nina so sweet and pretty,
I hear you crying saying what a pity.
Aunt Yvonne I know you are sad,
but I thank God for you because you always kept me glad.

To Aunt Barbara, Aunt Aretha and Aunt Bernetta thank you and I love you too. Here's a big hug and kiss to the three of you.
Aunt Joyce, Aunt Joyce so kind and sweet,
you are strong in heart but it's alright to weep.
Aunt Jean and Aunt Bessie I just have to mention, they are my grand mom sisters who love me so and gave me their full attention.

I'm with our God and I had to go, so calm down my family and take life slow, and one day I'll see you all again.

May God Bless You All, My Family and Kin.
[78]

Aunts, Cousins and Friends

Top row Aunt Pee Wee and Aunt Tiny

Bottom row front Aunt Jean, Aunt Johnny and Aunt Florence

Back row Chris Dooley, Molasses and Linda   Amber, Juan and E-Money
Front bottom: Family friend and my cousins LaJada, LaStarr and Sunni

[79]

To Cousins

Hey Cousins! I am just going to name a few, but remember I love each of you. I must start off with who I remember first: Tina, Stacy, James Jr, and Lynn. They were my first, like best friends.

To Darzell, Tiffany, Claudia, Ebony, and Hope my love for you will never change. Take care and do what's right and say your prayers each and every night.

Shey, Sunni, LaStarr, and Jada, my other girl cousins who I was like your big brother to, hold on to our good times and remember to go for the best.

Shantell, Princess, Brittany and Brejett my fine little cousins your dad has your back. Little Syria, Kristen, Dominique, and Ebony D., I miss all of you forever and a day. To G, my cousin Gerald, and Dee, who I call Ali, hold it down. Dontae, Darzell, Chris D., Patrick, and all the rest I know you all are wondering how this could be? Just stay strong and keep your head up high, and do what's right, I'll see you on the other side. Peace out...

To My Cousin Titus:

I know you are sad but there are so many things we just couldn't understand, but trust in God with all your heart and remember our good times together, **Love U Cuz...**

To all my cousins in Columbus, Ohio just to name a few Pastor Mark Hampton, Pastor Joyce Alexander, Darryl, Man, Tee, Aretha, Baby, Nancy and all my cousins in Macon, Georgia thanks cousin Tiny for that lovely song you sang, hey Henry and Neice thanks for coming. To all my others cousins whose names I didn't mention, remember to give God your full attention. **Love you E- Money**

Kenyette, Syria, Kristern, Ebony, LaJada, LaStarr, Claudia, Sunni, Tiffany & Hope

Souls That Were Touched

By Ilamani's Life

At the funeral it was announced by my Apostle Clarissa Dallas that it would be impossible for everybody to get up and speak on E-Money's behalf.

She instructed the people to contact me and to tell me how they feel and what they would like to say. What better way to let the world know what people really felt about my son than for me to write what was said by a few family members and friends.

We serve an awesome God and He places awesome people in our lives. I thank God again for my Apostle Clarissa Dallas along with my Pastors Roderick and L'aShawn Dallas.

These Are Words

Coming From

E-Money's

Family Members

And Friends

A Grieving Sister's Pain While Talking To God And Her Brother

When my brother (Ilamani) was first murdered it felt like a dream and in a way it still does. I mean I know that my brother is gone, but it is still hard to believe that I can't see him anymore or call him anymore. Lord, I know that death is a part of life and that we have to deal with the pain, but it hurts so much. I just wonder if I will ever see my brother again. Is there a life after? I am not questioning you Lord because I know that you are real, I just do not know what happens when we are gone. When we were kids my brother and I would question death, and we were both afraid of it. We would always ask you if we would still be a family and would we still have our same parents and grandparents and so on. Well, I'm not a kid anymore and my brother is dead and the question still stands. I trust in you Lord and I believe in what you say and if I could get just one sign of a miracle coming from you telling me that whenever I leave this world I will see my brother again, then I will be okay. I look at my mother (Evelyn) and it hurts me to see the pain in her soul. My brother was the first born and I know that she is dying inside just because of the way she love us all. When I look at my daddy (Leon) trying to be strong for all of us I say, "God help our family make it through." Looking at my youngest brother (LaJuan) I don't know what to say, it is hard because he never expresses his feeling, but I know he is in a dark place. I can't imagine what it was like for him to actually get a phone call from someone telling him that our brother had been shot and was lying in the street just two streets from where we stay. I know that he must be going through something that is too hard to explain. When he ran around the corner and saw our brother lying in the middle of the street with five bullets in him fighting for his life. I know it had to take him to a place far away, and all I can say to him is that our brother did not die alone, you were there with him and he knew it. That is the one thing that gives me peace knowing that when my brother took his last breath he knew he was with someone who loves him, and that someone was his brother LaJuan. This is the beginning of a lifelong of grieving. As I looked at E-Money in his casket I just have to believe (from the peace on his face) not only was my baby brother LaJuan there with him, Jesus was too. I thank you God for showing me your love for my brother E-Money.

Rest E-Money and I will see you when Jesus calls me.

To My Brother In Law I'm Going To Miss You

Even though I was just E-Money's brother in law it felt like we were more than that. We bonded immediately after meeting. It was as if E-Money and I were on the same page. We both liked to go all out for our favorite woman. He loved to help people out, period. E-Money was very family orientated. Family came first before anything. I loved him for that because that's the way I am. I wish we would have had more time to hangout, but I know you are watching my back still. E-Money always told me he was happy his sister found a guy like me. I'm just as happy because my wife's family makes me feel like I was born into their family. Even though we were just brothers by marriage, I'm going to miss you as though my real brother is gone.

Your Bro
LeShard

E-Money and Kenyette

Le'Shard and Kenyette

To My Brother E-Money From Juan

It's hard for me right now to find words that might bring comfort. All kinds of thoughts are running through my head. Words won't come out because I just can't believe you're dead. When I would get up in the morning you were the first person I would see coming to my door, just to make sure I was alright. I thank you brother for watching over me. You will always be right in my heart and I will never stop thinking of you. It's very difficult right now to express how I really feel in this book. But my love for you will always be. See you again in your new life.

Love your Bro Juan

A Grieving Sister-In-Law

My name is Amber and I'm engaged to LaJuan, E-Money's youngest brother. I've known E-Money for over 10 years; he was like a brother to me. He would come check on us, he loved his little brother LaJuan and LaJuan loved him. E-Money was a serious and charming person. His smile was bright and he was always smiling. He lived life to the fullest and enjoyed his family the most. Any and everybody that would come in contact with E-Money knew he was a realist. He was straight forward, if he didn't like something he would let you know and it was in a way that you knew, it was for your own good. He always complimented me and his brother as a couple, he was thoughtful like that. We were very close. He let us stay at his house in the beginning of our relationship. E-Money was a great person to have known. The pain that I feel losing a brother takes a piece of my life away every day. It was like ripping out something from my soul that I could not get back. I feel like it was nothing but jealousy. It was literally the most horrifying night I've ever experienced in my life. When E-Money was murdered it was traumatic. Trying so hard not to let the family see me cry that pain was overwhelming for me. The silence is so loud but there is an empty spot in our lives. We don't deserve that, no person does. I see E-Money in my dreams all the time. I look at his brother LaJuan every day, seeing and feeling the hurt he is going through. It was devastating to see his family grieve and hurt so openly. Being part of his family and trying to be strong for them was very hard. At that moment I begin realizing how much E-Money truly meant to all of us. I'm having a hard time dealing with his death and getting back to reality. When you lose something you cannot replace, you feel robbed. We didn't lose him he was taken away from us. One thing I can say is that E-Money left behind plenty of seeds planted to grow plenty fruit to better the world. We as a family will see to it that they harvest to produce the crop that he would want and be proud of! **REST IN PARADISE MY BRO BRO...PLEASE GOD, LET HIM JUST REST... FOREVER CHANGED, AMBER' LIL SIS.**

Unconditional Love To E-Money Your Sister Rhonda

Words I express couldn't tell the unconditional love that I have for you. When I received the phone call that night my heart hasn't beat right since. My big brother was the greatest brother a sister could ask for. Anytime I needed him he was always there for me.

E-Money named me Ro-Ro and I hated that name, but I liked it coming from him. My sister, Kenyette, and I always had to look out for our big brother when we went to hangout. He wouldn't let us do anything without him being there with us. He loved us that much that he would change his plans to protect us.

I would like to say to, Boo, the man that killed my brother. Your friendship was not genuine. My brother wouldn't have done that to you. He was real. You're going around saying you was scared. If that were true, then why did you come looking for him every day to hang out with him? I could think of a lot of mean things to say towards you, but that's not going to bring my loving brother back. Every day that goes by I think of that million dollar smile my brother had. I will always love u E-Money.

Love Always Your,
Lil sister Rhonda

My Son E-Money From Your Father Leon

There are no words for me to say. I'm sad and mad. This was something that I had no control of. If I did you would still be here. We had our father and son talks about the streets and how dangerous it can be. I believe you are in a better place although I wish you were still here. God only knows how much I miss you, son. I miss hearing you say to me, "what's up Pop's." I knew your heart and God does too, so I know I will see you on the other side. **Love Pop's**

Kenyette, E-Money & Mom   La'Juan and Pop's

To E-Money From Mama

I'm trusting in God for His promise. **John 14:3** reads: And if I go prepare a place for you, I will come back and take you to be with me that you also may be where I am." It was God speaking and saying, "E-Money's not dead I took him to a place where he can rest." It was E-Money's time and God knows what's best. I open my eyes and looked at the ceiling. I said to my God "thanks for that wonderful feeling." So son you see you had your fun, now your new life with God has just begun. I'm going to miss you and that's for sure. The love we shared as mother and son was real and pure. So rest in peace and I know I will see you again. Stop worrying about your kids, sister, China, and your brother. You're in the right place and you need no other. My love for you will never change. So enjoy your new life and save me a place and remember my love for you will never be erased. **Love, Your Mother**

[89]

To You Daddy I Love You So Much: Shavonte

How can I go on in life without the love of my daddy being in my life? My daddy is the world to me. As I sit back and look at your life and all that you have been through, I see now that God had his hands on you. He picked you up and carried you home. You left me, grand mom, and all your children and your family all alone.

One night I was lying in the bed trying to sleep.
I heard you say, "stop crying and baby don't you weep."
I know you want me to be strong and that I will do;
Daddy I just can't help myself I'm missing you.
I'm trying to work and go to school because I know that was one of your biggest rules. I will stay in college to seek all the knowledge. I love you daddy and I miss you so.

Love your daughter,
Ta-Ta

Shavonte age 14   **E-Money holding Shavonte at day one**

To You Daddy From Your Oldest Son EJ

Daddy you know you are my everything. I went away to Job Corp to get away from the streets and from distraction. Receiving a telephone call at 3:00 a.m. in the morning I knew that something was going on. I had several missed calls. When I called back home to see what was the problem, my mother told me she was on her way to come get me. Then I asked her why but she told me that she was going to tell me when she gets there. Two hours passed by and my mother, step dad and my sister finally arrived. I came to the office and my step dad grabbed me and walked with me and told me my dad was murdered. I looked at him then looked to the ground thinking to myself is this a dream. I couldn't believe this. As we all got in the car and headed back home my sister was crying and I was very sad. She told me what had happened. That whole day I kept wondering why my dad? I didn't talk to anyone that day. All I was thinking about was my dad. I knew that my grandmother which is his mother was very hurt and upset as well as our other family members. My dad was so funny and the coolest person ever. Sometimes he would get mad at me but later that day he would get over it. I didn't cry when he passed but I was so depressed and sad, but I knew my dad would want me to be strong. When I went to his funeral, that's when it hit me, I started crying because that was my last time for me to see him. Dad where ever you are, I just wish I could tell you one last time just how much I love you. Love your oldest son

EJ

[91]

To My Uncle Money From Little Chris

Words couldn't explain how close I was to my uncle. Me and my cousin E.J spent many weekends with him, enjoying games and laughing at my Uncle's jokes. I will never lose the feeling he left me with. The night of the shooting I was lying on my bed looking at the ceiling when there was a knock at the door. It was my grandmother yelling and screaming telling us my Uncle had been shot. My mother, step-dad, and grandmother hopped in the car and told me to go in the house. Instead I followed them to Wexford where I saw my uncle getting boosted into the ambulance. At that point I knew life for me or my family would never be the same. Uncle Money was a true comedian whether yelling at you or laughing with you, he kept all of us smiling and happy. I'm going to miss my uncle so much and I know my little brother and sister will too. We all know that he had much love for all of us. We miss and love you uncle Money!

Christopher, Serenity and Little LeShard

To Daddy From Manie

Daddy, I will miss playing your game and going outside with you. You made me laugh and you let me play with your dog. I miss you cause you made me smile and happy. I miss talking on the cell phone with you and riding in your truck. I miss you showing me how to write the number four. I miss looking at your fish. I miss you giving me a high five and when you tickle me. I am six years old and I love you infinity plus.

To my Daddy Love Azariah

I miss you daddy, I miss your voice and our time going to play with the dogs. I miss you daddy when you would call the house and bring us pizza. I miss you and want you to come back. Mama said that Jesus took you home. But daddy I miss you. We had so much fun together. I am seven years old and I will miss all the fun I had with you at the family picnic. I love you daddy, infinity plus infinity.

To U Daddy Love Your Wondering Why Daughter Sydnee

I didn't get to know you as well as my sisters and brothers, due to the distance relationship between you and mom. I do ask God daily as I wonder why? Just as we were getting to bond He allowed you to leave. I can say you showed me love when we were together, and you are the funniest and happiest dad in the world and I thank God that I look just like you. I will hold on to your last words. I remember just a month before your death when you told me you love me. Well Daddy, I love you too and I'm glad to be your daughter and I thank God for letting you and my mom bring me into the world. I just wonder why? As soon as we got close just a month later your life was over. I miss you. **Love you Forever Sydnee**

E-Money The Encourager
Coming From Pastor Tina

I would like to say praise the Lord to everybody. I'm Pastor Tina. I'm here to speak about E-Money whom I called E., E-Money was an awesome man of God. He had a personal relationship with God although you might not have seen it. I did and the Lord did also. Upon meeting him and talking to him he became my encourager. He was one of the most realest people I ever met. I believe that most of E-Money's associates, they knew him as a hard rock but as I got to know him his heart was soft but big and very real. He had no fakeness in him. He kept it one hundred. If he didn't like something or somebody he would keep it real. He wouldn't come right out and tell you that he didn't like you or be disrespectful; he just wouldn't be around you. He had a lot of respect for others. He had so much love for people and his family. I thank God daily for allowing me the opportunity of meeting him and getting a chance to know him. I became acquainted with E-Money through his mother Evelyn, who's a mighty woman of God. We met while discussing business. It turns out that she became my sister in Christ. I never had a sister before and God placed her in my life on time. I began to Minister to her children for over a period of three years. So I believe I can say the things I know about E-Money to be accurate. Every time he saw me he had a question pertaining to God. He was a young man who wanted to know about God but felt he wanted to come to God clean. I would tell him that God will take you just as you are, just come. I told him things of my past and how I came to God. I explained to him that there's no body prefect on earth. I kept it real with him. He asked me to hurry up and finish my church. He said when I finish remolding my church he would be the first one there. He wanted to become a Deacon. I laughed and told him he can be anybody he wanted to be just give his life over to God. He was my encourager when nobody else would encourage me or see God's vision for the church E-Money did. Well I'm still remodeling and the Lord took him home. I truly believe he would have been one of the first one's there. Most people look at people from the outside but God looks at us inside out. E-Money was a man of God and if you really knew him you would know that. E-Money will truly be missed, my me. I know that he's in a better place. He's with the Master. He's where we are destined to go to. With all that being said I will say, don't just take for granted people you might meet or see, and think it is a fly by night person. Stop and listen. Stop to hear. Stop and love. Stop and encourage others. Stop and lift one another up and this is what E-Money did. E-Money was about lifting people up when they were down. You never know who God will place in your life. It is truly an honor for me to speak on E-Money's behalf. He to me was an awesome man of God.

Love Pastor Tina.

Words About E-Money From Bishop JaVon

What a great brother to have known. Truly he was a man of God. Every time I came in contact with him he had a smile on his face and always complimented me on doing God's work or even my shoes. He had a good heart and I'm sure of his relationship with God. I say Rest In Peace My Brother.

Much Love Bishop

To E-Money The Love Of My Life China

Hey Baby, where do I begin, you are more than the love of my life you are also my greatest friend. Life should never be taken for granted now I can see. I never knew our relationship would end in this awful way. We promised one another we would never leave. I planned on keeping my mind. Now that you are gone what will I do? How do I go on? Getting up in the morning and going to bed at night, is the hardest without me in your arms and you holding me tight. I look at our baby Kameron and I begin to smile, and I thank you for leaving me a beautiful child. I don't know what to do or what to say; all I know is that I miss you so much. I love you then and I always will, so rest in peace until I will see you again.

Love You Yolanda (China)

How

I

Grieved

And

God's

Favor

LaJuan age 4

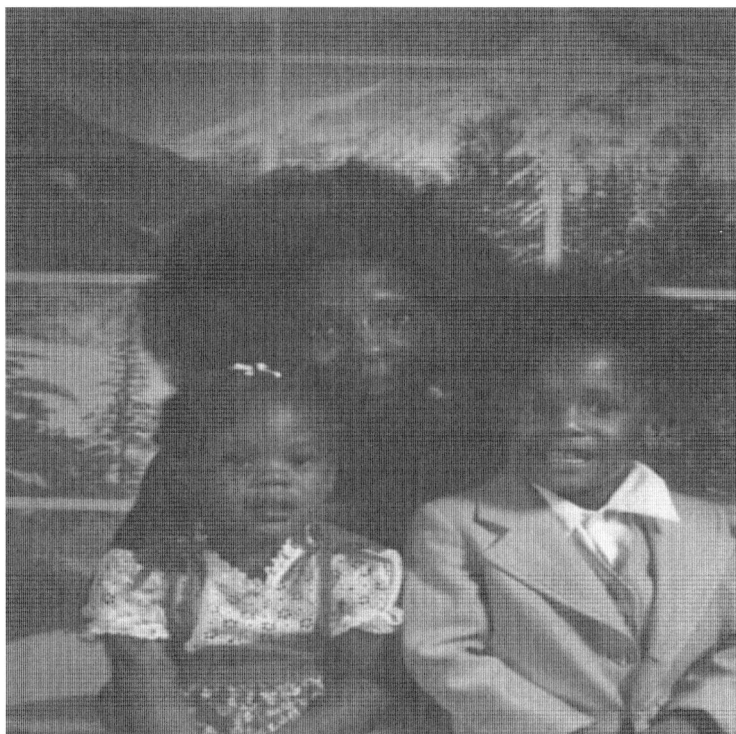

Evelyn with Kenyette 2 years old and E-Money 3 years old

From A Grieving Mother

Everybody grieves different, but there is only one helper that can clearly help us through and our help is our counselor, the Holy Spirit who lives inside of us. Let me introduce you to my savior while I grieve the death of my son E-Money.

St John 14:26 clearly tell us
The counselor which is the Holy Spirit who will teach us all things. Knowing this has helped me get started in trusting God. I began to ask God to show me his love in this. He answered me with **St John 3:16.** "If He didn't love us why did He let His son suffer?"

St John 3:16

For God so loved the world
that He gave His only begotten son
that whosoever believe in Him
should not perish
but have eternal life.

This is one of the scriptures which kept me sane. While grieving I wasn't thinking clear. I needed to keep my focus on God but my focus kept going to the boy, Boo, who murdered my son. I wanted one minute alone with him. I knew that wasn't my character but that's all I could think of is getting even with him. My thoughts were getting out of control when I first began to grieve the death of my son. I had so much hate inside of me and I truly wanted to get rid of it, but it wasn't going anywhere. I know the Lord and I love him with all my heart, so why was I thinking like that? I began to pray but no words would come out my mouth. Every time I tried to open my mouth to pray, my mind wouldn't let me. So I just meditated on the strength from the Lord. Truly speaking I really didn't know what was going on with my body. I just knew I hated Boo, the man that murdered my son and it seemed like I hated the world. I wanted to pray but I had no words. God is so awesome. When I did speak, it was a poem that God gave to me.

In God's Care

These words came out my mouth and it was a poem

I wonder how my heart will be healed
Knowing it's real my son was killed
I believe in God without a doubt
But all I can do is scream and shout
I try to pray morning, noon, and night
God won't let me He's getting my heart right
I toss and turn trying hard to go to sleep
God whispered in my ear, "it's alright to weep"
Now it's time to mend your heart
I know your love for me will never part
I begin to pray

Matthew 6:8-13
Our Father in heaven,
Hallowed be Your name.
Your kingdom come.
Your will be done
On earth as it is in heaven.
Give us this day our daily bread.
And forgive us our debts,
As we forgive our debtors,
And do not lead us into temptation,
But deliver us from the evil one.
For Yours is the kingdom, and the power, and the glory forever.
Amen."

Matthew 6:14-15
14. "For if you forgive men their trespasses, your Heavenly Father will also forgive you. 15. But if you do not forgive men trespasses, neither will your Father forgive you trespasses.
Look at God:
Lesson one had to be learned

God will never leave me, He's always with me, I had to remember what **St John 3:16** meant when Jesus died on the cross for our sins. He left the Holy Spirit which lives inside of us. So if I needed assurance of where my son is, God has shown it to me again. Whosoever believes in Him should not perish but have eternal life.

I knew my son believed in Jesus Christ and that is my confirmation from God. Now I know my son is truly in His care.

So **lesson one** is to trust God with all your heart and lean not to your own understanding and in all your ways acknowledge Him and He will direct your path. **(Proverbs 3:5-6) Lesson two** had to be learned. I knew that I had to stay grateful to God who is and always will be the head of my life. It took my attention back to **Matthew 6:** *Jesus is our daily bread and I must eat on His word.* He also tells us in His word to forgive and He will deliver us from the evil one. I knew I had to forgive Boo for murdering my son. I had to get rid of that evil spirit in me. I knew it wouldn't be easy but I had to trust in God no matter what and obey His Word. I know it is hard to forgive somebody when you know you didn't do anything to them. But we must think about God and how many times God has forgiven us.

So **lesson two** is to be obedient to the word of God and wait on the Holy Spirit to guide you. So praise God with your whole heart.

Stay obedient and grateful.

I needed someone positive to talk to. People kept coming to me talking about their negative experiences of when they lost a loved one. I know everyone grieves differently and I knew that God would handle me differently not because I'm special but because He deals with us individually-not based on someone else's experience. I'm going to continue to trust Him all the days of my life. God gave me this as I begin to feel down.

Psalms 9:1-2
I will praise You, O Lord with my whole heart; I will tell of your marvelous works. I will be glad and rejoice in You; *I will sing praise to Your name; O Most High.*
When you meet God for yourself, you don't need anybody else.

In God's Care

People kept coming to me telling me their negative experience of a loved one that died in their life. I know that God deals with each of us differently. He deals with us where we are. He will always take care of us, so only pick up on what will help you, when listening to a friend. Stay away from negative thinking. Talk to positive people like your pastors. If you don't have a Pastor, go to your neighborhood church. They will be glad to help you through your grief. If you are breathing, you are blessed so share the goodness of God whenever you get a chance. Don't just think about the sad times think about all the good times you had with your loved one. I can truly thank my Apostle Clarissa and Elder Gwen for all of their positive speaking and great words of encouragement. Without them talking and walking me through my loss I would not be writing this book. They helped me to trust and to depend on God no matter what. **That is lesson three.** Stay connected with some one positive. Lesson three **positive companies.** Share the goodness of God everywhere you go. **John 13:34** Jesus gives us a new command to love one another as He has loved us. So speak on God's marvelous works. Tell something good about your loved ones, daily. It's not going to be easy, but God will always be with you, just trust in Him. He is the only way possible for you to make it through. Trust Him in Jesus name I pray.

E-Money in Junior High with classmate Tina, his Mother, sister and brother LaJuan

To God

As I begin to think about all your goodness and where this book came from, and who gave it to me. I wonder why me? Why did you (God) choose me? Was this the only way for you to get my full attention? Almost every person I talk to that I know to be a positive thinker is telling me that somewhere I will get the glory. God I truly don't understand why this happen? "God I really miss my son." I know that you are perfect in all your ways and you make no mistakes. I need you to show me my lesson that you are teaching me. I feel the pain and I'm waiting for you to remove this hurt. My relationship with you has been on a personal level for a long time, but my relationship has never been at the level where it needs to be. Lord I need you to help me follow you all the way through. I know it was you who placed this book in me. I'm slipping and I don't know where I'm slipping to. You said in your word that you will never leave or forsake me. I know that you are with me I feel your presence. I need you to take full control of my mind, body and soul. "Help me" to walk within the fullest of your righteousness. Right now I really don't understand what's going on, but I do know that you are in full control. I'm going to stay in your presence until you give me a clear answer. Here I lay in your presence.

My prayer to my Heavenly Father will be for Him to help me to put on the full armor in doing His will. Teach me all I need to know to stay obedient to Him and His word. In the name of Jesus I pray. Amen

Let God Be God When Grieving

There are many different stages a person goes through while grieving. My first stage, I believe, was shock and disbelief. My life was meaningless. I wanted to know how I could possibly survive. Life to me as I knew it was over, I was overwhelmed and in total denial. How can I make it through another day or do I even want to make it through another day? I was hoping this to be a dream. Having to face the various situations and experiences life presents to you when we least expect it. But I just don't want to face reality. Blame, anger, and hate, all three was knocking at my door. Anger or hate has no limits. My natural feelings were hurting and I didn't understand the pain. All I knew was that I'm mad, sad, and I'm angry at the world. Where is God? Blaming myself and asking God what did I do wrong? I hated myself because I felt that I could have done something.

My emotions were out of control. I was beginning to become depressed. Depression was all around me. I felt so empty, lost in my body not knowing which way to turn. I saw myself withdrawing from life. I was at a level of depression that was getting deeper and deeper than you could ever imagine. I had lost grasp of my life. My husband wanted me to get professional help. I asked God was this feeling that I'm experiencing going to be permanent? I asked God to help me maintain my mind. I asked God to get me out of this stage of depression. My God faithfully answered my prayers. We must always remember who we can call on in the midnight hour. We can always call on King Jesus Christ He's never too tired. He is our key to healing. We must trust Him enough and call on Him. Guess what? He is waiting on your call.

God Has Placed Me On A Rock.
He Is My Solid Foundation

Only what God allows can come into our life. There is nothing impossible for God, He gives us the victory. Our help comes from the almighty God. I must keep repeating that over and over in my mind. I must trust in God with all my heart and stand on His Word. I wasn't feeling what the Word says, but I had to surrender to God and submit myself unto the Holy Spirit, listening and letting God speak. I knew I had to trust in God no matter what. I knew I needed to call on God every second in a day to build my faith in Him. Knowing that faith without works is dead. I felt like I was standing alone but at the same time I could feel the presence of God. But I wanted to see him. How many of you know we serve an awesome God. He began to give me what I wanted. He began to show me a vision of where my son was and who he was with.

My first vision was a flame of light with my son's face and written in the background, **In God's Care**. I didn't believe what I had seen at first, I thought it was just my imagination playing tricks with my mind. Then the Holy Spirit spoke to me the second time and said, didn't you say you wanted to see him. My Father is real. God does not have time to play tricks with your mind. **St. John 14:6** Tells me: Jesus said to him, "I am the way, the truth, and the life. No one comes to the Father except through Me." Also another scripture says in **1 Corinthians** "He who begins a good work in me will complete it until the day of Christ Jesus." I heard a voice say, "I will never leave or forsake you, I will remain with you." I can rest now and trust that my son is in His care. Remembering **St. John 15:5** "I am the vine, you are the branches. He who abides in me, and I in him, bears much fruit: for without me you can do nothing." When I first read that scripture it had no meaning to me, so let me explain it to you.

Jesus is telling us that He is the root and the key to His Father who also is our Father. If we, who are the branches, obey His (God) word meaning for us to be obedient. Then we can bear much fruit, meaning our life will prosper. My heart stayed comforted for a while, but my mind kept trying to take me to a place of darkness when all God was showing me was light. I knew that I had to take one day at a time and I couldn't let that devil in for a minute. I knew the devil was trying to take me back to square one. But all I wanted to do was see my son laughing and having a good time. I just want to tell him one more time how much I love him. God will always give us what we need when we need it. That's when another vision came to me from God. This vision was different from the others. It was in more detail. God took me down memory lane. Oh how awesome is our God. He let me see the greatest love a mother and a son could have. I went back to the day of my son's birth, which was one of the happiest days of my life. That was God's first step in lifting up my mind, body soul and spirit. God began to heal me day by day. My son had been dead now for two days and I had to handle his home going.

I thank God my Heavenly Father for all you have done for me. I know with the help of the Holy Spirit that lives inside of me, I will get myself together soon. In Jesus Holy name Amen

It Ain't Over Until God Says It's Over

It was my first day back to work, after a non- stop belief of God's favor on my life. It was still hard for me to understand why my son was dead or why he had to die. All I know is that we all are only here temporarily. I also know that our God is perfect in all His ways and I must trust Him no matter what. As I sit at work in my clothing store trying to clear my head, God releases His power in me to a degree that I knew it wasn't anybody but God. I never stopped praying to God since the first day of my son's death. I didn't want to pray sometimes but the love that I have for God and the love He has for me kept me praying. I just had to, not really understanding why? I just did. I know clearly that prayer is the key in life, and faith opens the door. I never stop praying although sometimes words wouldn't come out my mouth. It wasn't my choice, words just wouldn't come out. I knew I had to stay connected with God somehow. I remember my mother saying prayer is the key to heaven and faith unlocks the door. Prayer without faith is like trying to open a locked door with the wrong key. Wisdom like that always came from my mother but not this time while battling a stage of dementia. She can't give me any advice or any encouraging words. I had to remember everything I was told by my mother about God and focus on the way I think she would have given me guidance. I believe the first thing she would say is God never allows a person to handle more than they can take. I felt like I was dying inside and I had no reason to live. Second by second and minute by minute, I felt my life drifting away. I loved my daughter Kenyette and my son LaJuan just as much as I love E-Money but I wasn't thinking clear. I had forgotten all about my husband and grandchildren and God knows I would never want to leave them. My thinking wasn't rational. I've heard of people giving up on life after they lost a love one, but I never thought it was a possibility that they had no control of their thinking. I didn't want to give up but it seemed as I was lost mentally. I was invaded by unfamiliar feelings in my stomach and my mind. I strongly believe in the Bible and everything I was taught. I know that God is omnipotent meaning all powerful. I also know that in the Bible that **St John 10:10:** tells us that Satan comes to kill, steal, and destroy. I had to keep telling myself, that it ain't over until God says it over. God loves me, you and my son no matter what. I had to learn to let go of the past and accept the future. God is ready to do a new thing in me. I can hear Him saying get ready for change. Don't be afraid my child to move forward and let me make some new adjustment in your life. A small adjustment can make a big improvement. When God is ready to improve a person's life you must be open for change. I knew my life had changed because my son E-Money was no longer here on earth with me anymore. I'm wondering, "How could I be open for change?" Then a voice whispered in my ear and said, "You are trying to hold on to your son, Release him. He's in my care now. I'm going to release a book to you. Many will know the story of E-Money's life here on earth and God's favor of a grieving mother. Can you trust me?" When I heard that I didn't understand or know what to do. Days went by and one night I dreamed that I wrote a book. The next morning very early I got up and this is the beginning of my book. God gave me a story to tell of the life with my son E-Money here on earth from beginning to end. I know that this book will be a blessings to many.

Thank You God for your many blessing you have placed in my life. As you know I will praise you all the days of my life. I ask that if you are reading this book that you ask God to keep you in His perfect peace. Always remember:

Philippians 4:13
You can do all things through Christ Jesus who strengthens you.

[109]

The Murder

And

E-Money's

Last Days

On Earth

About The Murderer

Talking about the murder is a nightmare that will never end for me. I do want the world to know that my son was murdered in cold blood. So here's what I can tell you about the murderer. His street name is Boo. I think it would be only fair to him for me not to give his real name. I have only known Boo for about four years, personally. My children knew him much longer from school and the neighborhood. My children never hung out with the neighborhood kids while growing up. They had enough cousins and family members to play with. Plus, as a family, we did a lot of family things together. E-Money was a working man most of his life so he didn't have that much time to hang out. Boo never had a job out of the four years I knew him. He would come to E-Money's house every day when E-Money came home from work ready to hang. E-Money lived two doors down from my house so I knew just about everybody who came to his house.

E-Money loved to barbeque, so he would have a lot of bar-b-ques at his house. E-Money strongly believed that Boo knew who the persons were that murdered his cousin, Double O and one day might slip-up and say something wrong. That was his first reason for ever hanging with him. Later E-Money moved off my street, he moved about four streets away and I no longer could see what was happening or who was visiting his house. He was grown and was doing good on his own. I was just a busy body mother only wanting the best for my children. I do know that E-Money didn't sell drugs or steal, he was what I call "doing his thing," but minding his own business. He liked to have a good time all the time. E-Money introduced Boo to the girl that Boo is dating currently. I was told through rumors that Boo moved in with her immediately. She was the first girlfriend he had since dating his baby mama, who has moved on with her life. A lowlife is what he was known as in the neighborhood just hanging from corner to corner and door to door trying to get his high and get his drink on. His new girlfriend gave him a place to stay not knowing his background. After being with Boo for a while, she was telling everybody in the neighborhood that she was planning on leaving him anyway. That's not a rumor that came right out of her mouth and I heard it. He couldn't even help her pay a bill. So as you see it's really not too much that I can say about the murderer. (I would say thanks to E-Money, for finding Boo a girlfriend and a place to stay). He just hung in the streets looking for something to get into.

E-Money has a family who loves him and he could always get a job. E-Money believed in working. Boo believed in the streets and waiting for the next person to support his habits. Boo would come looking for E-Money as soon as E-Money came home from work. That was Boo's every day habit. Why he murdered my son, only Boo and God knows. People are saying Boo was afraid of E-Money but that's not true. Boo knew he couldn't beat E-Money in a fair fight, so I guess he took the coward way out. Most street guys that drink on a daily basis have arguments and disagreements, but they don't go around killing each other. Boo proved to me that he really is the lowlife door to door street boy that everybody in the neighborhood called him. E-Money looked at Boo as needing a real friend. They had some disagreements and arguments, but at the end of the day, they were still friends. E-Money never would have shot Boo. Boo shot my son five times and had the nerve to say it was an accident. As I tell you this story my heart hurts. I cry out to God to have mercy on his soul. I also pray that I will see myself forgiving Boo in my lifetime in Jesus name I pray.

Gerald and E-Money

The Week before E-Money's Death

We had our family reunion a couple weeks before E-Money's death. I thank God that he allowed E-Money to enjoy a wonderful weekend with his entire family. Our family reunion was up north at a resort, we stayed there three wonderful days. E-Money was one of the first to get up every morning to take his children to breakfast and swimming, he spent his quality time with them first and then he let them enjoy their cousins while visiting his cousins here from out of town. That was a weekend that was planned by God for E-Money's home going, he enjoyed the food and he was so happy to see a lot of his family members from out of town. At night before he went to bed he would come to my hotel room and talk to me and his daddy, we agreed saying how we needed to do this more often. I told him that I would give a big family dinner as a start, we laughed and joked and had a great time together. We talked about his job and he talked about my clothing store, he would always call me Mrs. Jefferson moving on up. He had been on his job for over two years and he wanted to get his own business one day like his dad and I. When the reunion weekend was over and he went back to work the following Monday, he was laid off. He called me on his way home and he was sad, he loved his job and he loved to work. He said they would be calling him back in two weeks, but he was still sad, I cheered him with jokes and asked him to come work with me, he came straight to my store and finished out the day with me. I truly believe God prepared us for E-Money's home going because we had the happiest days together in the last month of his life. E-Money and I always talked; he loved for me to pray with him daily. E-Money loved me so much and I love him just as much, he would always say mama I don't know what I would do if anything ever happened to you. I would laugh and say boy don't worry about me, just be careful out there with Boo and that crowd, he said, "Mama, I don't hang like that no more, I got a new born baby now." Just as we finished talking E-Money wasn't there with me two hours before Boo came up to the store, he saw E-Money's truck parked in the parking lot so he came in to see why E-Money wasn't at work. E-Money told Boo he was laid off for a couple weeks. Boo came back around closing time and they both left together. That continued all week. Boo would come there just minutes after E-Money and I would arrive for work. Three days before E-Money's death, China and E-Money gave a barbeque at their house and he announced Boo as the godfather of their three week old baby boy. I believe that to be a joke. My grandson will be raised by Godly godparents, so that was a joke. E-Money had no idea that Boo was nothing but a low down dirty cold blooded murderer. Many of the guys in the crowd would tell me to talk to E-Money about hanging with Boo, because they said Boo was a snake and a back biter. I told E-Money what I was told and also who informed me of these thing about Boo. E-Money would smile like he always did and say, "Boo is straight, mama. Stop worrying, Boo straight." How wrong would he be?

The Day Of E-Money's Death

The day of his death we talked about the goodness of God and all that God had done for him. He told me that he prayed to God every night to change his life around for the good. He was so happy about his new born son, Kameron, and planning his marriage to China. I told him to trust in God, and God will do anything you ask. While we were talking and getting ready to close, guess who showed up? Boo. There was a barbeque around the corner on Wexford and he came to tell E-Money. That was about 4:45 p.m. Monday. According to his fiancé E-Money went home first and spent time and played with their new born baby boy. China said he watched TV then he left. To China's understanding E-Money was going to the store. He hung out for a while and then went to the store. While leaving the store E-Money called China on his cell phone telling her he was going back to the barbeque to pick up a plate and come home. That was China's last conversation with E-Money.

E-Money his Mother Evelyn and his brother LaJuan

What Led To E-Money's Death

Lynn, who was one of the witnesses, was at the barbeque sitting in a van with Boo and some other guys. Lynn told me that he saw Boo with a gun and was telling him to put the gun away. He said he had been shot before and he didn't like to be around guns. Lynn said Boo didn't listen to him. Lynn said he saw E-Money driving down the street coming back from the store and he told E-Money that Boo had a gun. E-Money and Boo had hung together every day so Lynn thought Boo would listen to E-Money. Boo still wouldn't put the gun away. Lynn said E-Money kept telling Boo to put the gun away. Lynn said he turned his head because he had to take a leak (urinate) at the back of the truck, so he said that he didn't see Boo shoot E-Money but he knew that Boo shot him because Boo was the only one with a gun. If Lynn was so afraid of Boo having a gun in the first place do you believe that Lynn would have turned his back to urinate during a disagreement? Why Lynn didn't tell the whole truth only him and God knows.

My son was shot five times and they said no one saw anything. The other witness Mike was in the van with Boo. Mike was sitting in the front seat and Boo was sitting in the back. Mike, said that he heard Boo and E-Money arguing about putting the gun away and Mike then said that he saw E-Money walk over to Boo, he heard a slap, and then gun shots. If two people are arguing and one had a gun and you are in the middle just sitting, wouldn't you be looking at their every move? Mike, Lynn, and T-Bone saw Boo shoot my son. I thought they all were like family but I see now I was wrong. I thank them for speaking up but I wish they would have told the whole truth. They didn't even stay around to tell me what happened. They all knew where I live. My question is could it be possible that my son might be alive today, only if they would have come and got me or just called. Somebody called my youngest son, on his cell phone and told him his brother was lying in the street shot.

LaJuan With His Brother

When LaJuan saw his brother shot up in the street on Wexford, he could only hold him in his arms. E-Money was covered with towels and people were standing around crying and screaming. One person later told me that she was a nurse and she saw the witness move E-Money's body so Boo could get in his car and leave the scene. The witness said E-Money fell in front of Boo's girlfriend's car and when Boo was getting ready to take off they didn't want Boo to run over E-Money. How dirty and cruel could Boo be? The nurse said she told them to call 911. Brenda a friend and a member of the same church I attend said she was driving home that night and she heard gun shots; she knew that her son hung in that area so when she saw the crowd of people she thought it might be her son. When she got there she saw my son on the ground, she said she began to pray to God with all the power she had in her. She also said she asked God to forgive him for all his sins, and she told him to hold on. She had a friend with her that was a nurse and she helped the other nurse place towels and cover E-Money up. Brenda stated that she kept talking to E-Money telling him to hold on, and focus on God. LaJuan who is the brother of E-Money was there but he really doesn't remember too much about that night, all he remembers is holding E-Money waiting on the EMS truck and praying for his brother's life. While holding E-Money in his arms he believed E-Money took his last breath. LaJuan held him until the police and EMS took and placed him in the ambulance. Boo's two brothers T-Bone and Way were there also. When LaJuan came they left. They knew what their brother had done because T-Bone was there when Boo shot E-Money; he left the scene and came back with his younger brother Way to see if E-Money was going to make it. Everybody out there knew that Boo had shot E-Money but nobody said a word to LaJuan. I guess that was the best thing because it's no telling what would have happened. So I see God was there with my spiritual eye. LaJuan stayed with E-Money until the ambulance arrived.

About The Witness

The witnesses wanted to tell what happened but they both were on parole. They were afraid that they might go back to jail. I didn't really know how the system works; all I knew is that I wanted justice for my son's murder and I wanted it from the justice system not from the guys in the streets. I had a lot of offers from guys in the street to hurt Boo and his brothers that was not even on my mind. How do they think their mother would feel if one of them were hurt or killed? Two wrongs can never make a right, so that wasn't even a thought. Boo was on the run but we knew where he was all the time. People kept calling and telling us his every move. The witness came over to my house and told me and my husband what had happened. They were there when Boo shot E-Money. They told me detail by detail. They said E-Money was telling Boo to put away the gun, and it escalated into an argument. They said they saw Boo shoot E-Money, but they can't get involved because they were on parole. I told them that I would talk to the head detective but they will need to tell what happened, and they agreed.

Boo On The Run

While Boo was on the run, the detective was closing in on his every move. His brother, T-Bone was with him and they were getting their alibi together. Boo has an aunt that is a police officer and the rumor is that she was going to talk to the detective so Boo could turn himself in. I received a telephone call informing me that Boo was on his way to turn himself in. I called the detective and asked if Boo had turned his self in yet. He informed me, "not at that time." One hour later he called and said, "Yes it's true, Boo turned himself in."

The Detective and Prosecutor

I knew without a shadow of a doubt that Boo would get charged with first degree murder, because my son was shot five times, and the reason for his shooting was senseless. When I received the telephone call and the prosecutor told me that they were only charging him with second degree murder I wanted to faint. I asked him why and he said, "Because they knew each other and they were friends." That didn't sound right to me then, and it still doesn't sound right now. I was grieving my son's death and I just let the justice system slip that right past me.

Detective Sergeant Drew told me it was out of his hands. His job was to get the arrest regardless. I thank God for our Detroit Police and I would like to specially acknowledge Detective Sergeant Drew, who came to my home several times and took this case personal. He had gathered up enough information to know that Boo had committed the murder. I called the prosecutor back and he said he would make sure that Boo would do the max. I asked him what was the max and he told me 25 years plus two years for the gun. Even if Boo did life that still wouldn't bring E-Money back.

Boo should have gotten charged with first degree murder. Shooting a person five times is first degree. Only God and the justice system can answer that question of why wasn't he. But is the justice system doing their job or is some funny business going on. Boo's own brother T-Bone got on the witness stand and said Boo shot E-Money. The prosecutor asked him, how did he know Boo shot E-Money and he said Boo told him on his way when he turned his self in. That again was enough information for Boo to be charged with first degree murder not second. I wish the prosecutor would have done a longer investigation. I had to put all my trust in God, He's in full control. I wish I knew then what I know now. They caught me at a vulnerable time to explain to me that the charge would be 2nd degree. I was too busy grieving my son's death that I couldn't think. By the time I had time to think. Boo pled guilty to second degree.

Boo Pleads Guilty

Everything happened too fast. Boo turned himself into the police three days after he shot and killed my son. About three days after E-Money's funeral we had to go to court. I really didn't have time to think. I was still in a vulnerable mood. They bonded Boo over from 36th District Court to Frank Murphy Court and charged him with a fire arm possession and second degree murder. Why didn't I get a chance to speak on my son's behalf? What happened to a mother's rights? My rights and the rights of E-Money were taken away. Was it because they just wanted to get the case over? Was my son just a nobody to them? Did Boo snitch on somebody to get this special treatment? Was there foul play? So many questions were running through my head. I asked the prosecutor how much time would Boo get if he pled guilty. He told me 25 to 30 years. About a week later a new prosecutor took over the case and I never saw the detective again. The new prosecutor was a lady and she said Boo's lawyer wanted to go for self-defense. Could you believe that? Where was E-Money's weapon? You shot a person five times and you say self-defense, no way. The prosecutor said she wasn't going to let that happen. I couldn't believe Boo would even try saying it was self-defense. I prayed for God to just let this be over. I couldn't take it anymore. Within a week, Boo had pleaded guilty to all counts. He was sentenced to 17 to 30 years. I'm not satisfied with the 17 to 30 but I wouldn't even be satisfied if Boo would have gotten 100 years because that can't bring Ilamani (E-Money) back.

God is always in full control. He will work it out. We must Trust In Him no matter what. He will always be with you. Life is a gift from God. I will let God be God and I will be His willing vessel. I will let the Holy Spirit control me. Thank you... Amen.

My Prayer to Boo and For Boo

I pray that God keep you in His perfect peace. People ask me why do I pray for you and the answer to that question is simple and easy. You made a mistake now you must ask God to forgive you and save your soul. My heart hurts every day for E-Money to come back to me, I miss him so much but I know that is impossible for him to come back. I do know that I will see him again because the bible tells me. I remember you calling me mom and telling me you wish your family had the same love for you that I had for E-Money. You also asked me in the courtroom if I would forgive you someday. The Bible tells me that I must forgive my trespassers and if I forgive, my Heavenly Father will surely forgive me. I know that I will always remember that you shot and murdered my son, but the key to forgiving is to start the process and to let God do the rest. My answer to you is yes I will forgive you. But God is the forgiver. I say to you find God, trust in the Lord while you are in prison and ask God to direct your path. God loves you just the much as He loves me. I pray that you get connected with Him. You have nothing but time on your hands. Use it for your good. Again I say may God keep you in His perfect peace. Read the Bible and pray you have a chance to change.

[120]

God

Continues

To

Lay

His

Hands

On

Me

Who Is God?

As I come to the end of my book. I begin to think about all that God has done for me in my traumatic situation. This question came to my mind. Why does God love us so much, even when we aren't loveable?

Exactly Who Is God?

We learn as a child that God is invisible. We learned that He can see everything we do. We also learned that God lives in heaven and He created us along with the heaven and earth. We know that God is good and His mercy endures forever. We also know that God is worthy to be praised.

How do we know these things? Is it because our parents, grandparents, teacher, or maybe a friend initially introduced us to this way of thinking? Have you ever picked up the Bible to learn about who God is for yourself? If not let today be your first time in learning the real deal about who God is? Some might say why does it matter? Others may say I'll take your word. Well I say God is the greatest person I have ever met and I can't help but want to introduce Him to the world. So go get that Big Bible off your shelf that has been sitting there collecting dust. (smile). If you don't have a Bible in your home go to any local church I'm sure they will assist you.

Step 1.

Whenever you begin to read your Bible, always start off with prayer asking God to give you understanding and a clear mind. Let your heart be ready to receive, what thus says the lord.

Step 2.

Always have a pen, paper, and a highlighter available so you can take notes, and highlight any questions. When reading you will always have questions, you can easily go back to get a better understanding later. Make sure you put the date on all your notes.

Step 3.

Now find a quiet place in your house so you can enjoy the most wonderful time of your life. Getting to know Who God Is? You are now on your way to getting acquainted with God.

The purpose of this book was also written to help you discover for yourself who God is and what He is really like? He is longing to become our friend. He is waiting for us to respond to His love and enter into fellowship with Him. In order for us to come in relationship or fellowship with Him we must first come to know Him for ourselves.

Let's get started.

Knowing God is what Christianity, and religion is all about. The best way to get acquainted with God is to read His word. The Bible tells us in **St. John 1: 1-5** 1. In the beginning was the Word, and the Word was with God, and the Word was God. 2. He was in the beginning with God. 3. All things were made through Him, and without Him nothing was made that was made. 4. In Him was life, and the life was the light of men. 5. And the light shines in the darkness, and the darkness did not comprehend" it. That is the eternal word. Study this scripture and ask God to help you absorb the words and their meaning into your mind, body, heart and soul. You are now on your way to understanding Who God Is? And His many wonderful ways in helping you to be what He will have you to be. But first you must study His word and put your trust in Him. As I grieved the loss of my son I learned who God really is to me. He is the Lilies of the valley; He is my bright and morning star. There's nothing too hard for Him. He is **El-Shaddai,** the all mighty God. He is the Great I Am. He is **Jehovah Shalom** my Prince of Peace. I thank God for the peace of mind that so rests upon me. God is **Jehovah Jireh** my provider. He provided me with a new heart at the Alter. Life will make you feel like there's no way out, but God He is my **Jehovah Shammah,** He never left me. He is the lord that is always present. I can go on and on and on.

In God's Care

God has the capacity of speaking things into existence.

Genesis 1: Teaches on the history of God's creation. God demonstrated who He is by His power and love. With only a spoken word God created everything around us.

Genesis 1:3-5 reads: 3. And God said, Let there be light: and there was light. 4. And God saw the light, that it was good: and God divided the light from the darkness. 5. And God called the light day, and the darkness He called night. And the evening and morning were the first day.

Each day God created something and on the seventh day He rested and blessed it. Read Genesis chapter 1 and 2 and you will learn more about God's creation. Now on the six day, God created man.

Genesis 1:27 tells us that God created man in His own image. **Genesis 2:7** tells us that the Lord God formed man of the dust of the ground, and breathed into his nostrils the breath of life, and man became a living soul. As you read on down you will see that God formed every beast of the field, and every fowl of the air; and brought them to Adam so he can name them. **Genesis 2:21** God caused a deep sleep to fall upon Adam, and he slept: and He took one of his ribs, and closed up the flesh. 22. The rib, which the Lord God had taken from man, He made a woman, and brought her unto Adam. **Genesis 3:20** Tells us that Adam called his wife Eve; because she was the mother of all living.

Now I thought I would give you your first lesson on where we came from and who created the universe. If you read Genesis chapter 1-3 you will learn all about God's creation and where sin started. Take notes and write down what God created from day one to six. That will be your first assignment. Once you study and learn that. You are on your way to understanding Who God Is?

I pray that you continue to read your bible and study to show yourself approved. Bible Study and Sunday School at a local church is a good place to start.

The Goodness Of God

Just by looking at a person on the outside you can't determine what they are really going through. I'm hurting and all at the same time, I'm happy. I know that the loss of my son will always be on my mind, and the feeling of sadness to a degree will always be with me. God welcomes each of us into a relationship so we can personally get to know Him. He is approachable and He is concerned about us. God is a forgiving God. We are made right in God's sight. God understands all the elements of a situation including the past, present, and our future. We don't have to inform Him God knows everything in advance.

Psalms 145:17-21

17. The Lord is righteous in all His ways,
Gracious in all His works.
18. The Lord is near to all who call upon Him,
To all who call upon Him in trust,
19. He will fulfill the desire of those who fear Him;
He also will hear their cry and save them.
20. The Lords preserves all who love Him,
But all the wicked He will destroy.
21. My mouth shall speak the praise of the Lord,
And all flesh shall bless His holy name
Forever and ever.

Jesus, the Son of God, paid for our sin with His death on the cross. He rose from the dead and offers us His forgiveness. What a mighty God we serve. As I think about God's goodness and all that He has done for me, my soul cries out **Hallelujah! Thank you Jesus**

How To Pray?

As I come to my close, I heard somebody say that they want to pray, but they don't know how? Well I was that same person, thinking that I didn't know how to pray. I would listen to how other people prayed and all the big words they used and how long they prayed. I never took the time out to think on what I had to say to God. I was so busy listening to how others prayed that I didn't take the time out to think about what it was I needed to pray for. Again my Pastors have pointed out that prayer is simply speaking to God talking to Him about whatever you want Him to improve in your life, although He already knows. If prayer is more than talking to God then I'm sure He will teach each of us what He wants us to know.

So the **first advice** I have to give to you is when you come to God, come real. He knows everything about us before we speak anyway and He knows what's on our mind, so just say it. He's not looking for us to come to Him with big words or long stories just tell Him what's on your mind. He's not going to jump out and bite you. He's here to help us through whatever we are going through, and to teach us of His goodness. So that we may live a prosperous life. Prayer is simply talking to God asking Him to guide you into His righteousness.

Prayer is coming to God as you are. When we pray, God already knows what we are in need of. He just wants us to communicate to Him on a daily basis, so we can develop a personal relationship with Him. Getting to know Him will be the best thing that could ever happen to you.

If you would please take out your Bible and turn it to 1 Timothy 2:

Reading from the inspirational study Bible: 1. Therefore I exhort first of all that supplications, prayers, intercessions, and giving of thanks be made for all men. 2. For kings and all who are in authority, that we may lead a quiet and peaceable life in all godliness and reverence. This scripture is telling us how to pray, read all of 1 Timothy 2:

I pray that you begin today talking to God daily. He will guide you all the way. Just start, God is longing to hear from you.

In God's Care

Bible Talk

Ephesians was written by Paul, an apostle of Christ Jesus by the will of God. While Paul's imprisonment in Rome (around the A.D. 60) he wrote several letters one speaking on the conduct of a believer. I will give you scriptures from the Bible, and real talk on how we should live. The book of Ephesians will be the first place where I will start.

Paul wrote to all believers that we are one family in Jesus, and we should act with love toward each other. He gives Christians instructions on how to "live a life of love." **Ephesians 1:2-8** reads 2. Grace and peace to you from God our Father and the Lord Jesus Christ. 3. Praise be to the God and Father of the Lord Jesus Christ, who has blessed us in the heavenly realms with every spiritual blessing in Christ. 4. For He chose us in Him before the creation of the world to be holy and blameless in His sight. In love 5. He predestined us to be adopted as His sons through Jesus Christ, in accordance with His pleasure, and will 6. To the praise of His glorious grace, which He has freely given us in the one He loves. 7. In Him we have redemption through His blood, the forgiveness of sins, in accordance with the riches of God's grace that He lavished on us with all wisdom and understanding. Now look at all the goodness God. God cherishes us. The more we know Him, the more we will understand Him. His love for us is unconditional.

As a believer we have a responsibility to love, honor, and respect each other. After reading this book your assignment for the babes in Christ is to get involved into a local church in your neighborhood and ask your leaders to place you where he or she feels you would be a blessing. Your service to our Lord Jesus in the church today is truly needed. Get ready for the time of your life. For believers, don't get too comfortable at just coming to church every Sunday doing the same thing do something different. God is waiting to turn this world around. We all as believers can participate with wisdom. Never put our self over a Pastor ask them what can we do to improve our love walk with helping in the church more. Love is the key. Let God use you daily.

Scriptures To Study and Learn

The book of Proverbs is the beginning of knowledge. Proverbs provide wisdom and guidance for living an obedient life. Study and live those scripture out and the blessing of the Lord will rest upon you.

Proverbs1: 7.

7. The fear of the Lord is the beginning of knowledge,
But fools despise wisdom and instruction.

Proverbs3:5-6.

5. Trust in the Lord with all your heart,
And lean not on your own understanding;
6. In all your ways acknowledge Him,
And He shall direct your paths.

Proverbs 15: 1-2.

1. A soft answer turns away wrath,
But a harsh word stirs up anger.
2. The tongue of the wise uses knowledge rightly,
But the mouth of fools pours forth foolishness.

As you read your bible start from the book of Proverbs each day. The book of Proverbs will help you make wise decisions. After learning from the book of Proverbs, you will be able to enjoy your bible. Be prepared to enter into a new dimension of faith, and a deeper revelation of God's love, and a renewed understanding that when you pray you will receive results.

If you don't have a church home to go to and receive the word, remember you can always join us. The doors of our church True Gospel Tabernacle Church will always be open for you. Let God use you for His Glory.

Something To Remember

Finally believing and trusting God is the best words I have to offer. As I finish up the last pages of my book the explosive power of God came over me as I knelt down, not in myself but in the spirit. A praise took place that was so Holy all I can say is I call Him Holy, His name is Holy, He is so Holy to me. I just want the world to know, I will praise God all the days of my life. Through my good times and my bad times, for He is worthy to be praised. I felt like giving up many times, but God grace and mercies kept me. He personally wrapped me up in His love and took care of me day by day. I will honor and serve God all the days of my life. I will also live my life by His agape love, and share it with others, as I have done most of my life. I now truly understand what the song means when it says, "If I had Ten Thousand Tongues I couldn't praise Him enough." That song is so true and real to me. I would like to take this time out in the closing of my book and Honor Our Father and Savior. From the book of Psalm

Psalm 66: 1-8

1. Make a joyful shout to God, all the earth!
2. Sing out the honor of His name;
   Make His praise glorious.
3. Say to God, "How awesome are Your works!
   Through the greatness of Your power
   Your enemies shall submit themselves to You.
4. All the earth shall worship You
   And sing praise to You;
   They shall sing praise to Your name." **Selah**
5. Come and see the works of God;
   He is awesome in His doing toward the sons of men.
6. He turned the sea into dry land;
   They went through the river on foot.
   There we will rejoice in Him.
7. He rules by His power forever;
   His eyes observe the nations;
   Do not let the rebellious exalt themselves. **Selah**
8. Oh, bless our God, you peoples!
   And make the voice of His praise to be heard

In God's Care

1. O God, You are my God;
   Early will I seek You;
   My soul thirsts for You;
   My flesh longs for You
   In a dry and thirsty land
   Where there is no water.
2. So I have looked for You in the sanctuary,
   To see Your power and Your glory.
3. Because Your lovingkindness is better than life,
   My lips shall praise You.
4. Thus I will bless You while I live;
   I will lift up my hands in Your name.
5. My soul shall be satisfied as with marrow and fatness,
   And my mouth shall praise You with joyful lips.
6. When I remember You on my bed,
   I meditate on You in the night watches.
7. Because You have been my help,
   Therefore in the shadow of Your wings I will rejoice.
8. My soul follows close behind You;
   Your right hand upholds me.
9. But those who seek my life, to destroy it,
   Shall go into the lower parts of the earth.
10. They shall fall by the sword;
    They shall be portion for jackals.
11. But the king shall rejoice in God;
    Everyone who swears by Him shall glory;
    But the mouth of those who speak lies shall be stopped.
    As we honor our Lord together
    always remember.   He is worthy to be praise.

Words from Julius Justice of Urban City Publishing

Meeting Evelyn and her family was one of the best things to ever happen in my life. When I met her I owned a call center selling products such as AT&T and other long distance products. Evelyn came to the company and right away we clicked. That was 15 years ago. I would say within a month or so of her working there, she became our sales manager and brought along most of the young people in her family as well as their friends to work there. We had between 30 and 40 employees and many of them were people that she recruited and they were all excellent sales people. Some were better than others, but they were all good because she trained them. It was a booming time for us and an excellent training ground for the young people. This was also during the early days of my publishing business and she was also very supportive of that. She actually met and recruited radio personality Frankie Darcell and brought her up to the office. Frankie and I ended up doing a book together. During this time E-Money was also working there and I can honestly say that he was one of those young people that came to the company and excelled. As I was working on this book, doing my part, I would read from people who stated that he was the ultimate gentleman, and he was. He was a great guy. Very positive and respectful. He was always asking if there was anything that he could do to help out, in addition to his usual job. There are many positive black males from Detroit that are gunned down every year and many people who don't know them, assume the wrong things after their death. Hopefully after reading this book will help change that mentality.

Final Thoughts

Encouraging Words: I'm Blessed and Highly Favored

All that God is and all that God has may be received through prayer. Everything and anything we need to fulfill our purpose on earth is available to us through prayer. If it had not been for the Lord on my side I don't know where I would be. He picked me up and turned me around and place my feet on solid ground. I will bless the Lord at all times. I will praise Him all the days of my life. I will continue to speak of His goodness. I will walk upright in all His ways. I have been called to stand on God's word no matter what. I had to switch my way of thinking and "think" Godly. I had put away my pride and latched on to wisdom. Wisdom comes in our lives to help us understand righteousness. I had to release my feelings and let God work through me, forgetting about my low self-esteem and let God do what He wants to do with me, and in me. I surrendered and let God have His way in me. I had to choose to do it God's way and not my way. I say to everyone that's reading this book, God loves us more than we could ever know. He will keep on loving you. We can't erase our future nor can we erase our past. We need to let go and let God be in control of our lives. When we do this, we are led to live a righteous life. A righteous walk with our Lord places us in a position of understanding His will in our lives. When you understand that God's will is being done in your life, you too, just as I can say "To God be the Glory," even in trying times.

In God's Care

Personal Notes

In God's Care

In God's Care

In God's Care

In God's Care

About The Author

Evelyn Murphy, a woman of righteousness and love for all. She has a heart of gold and it's noticeable. Born and raised in Detroit Michigan. Where she met and married Leon Murphy who has been the love of her life for over 30 years. She's a mother of three children the late Ilamani her oldest son, Kenyette and LaJuan, grandmother of nine and a role model too many. She loves her family and she loves helping others.

Writing this book is truly a gift from God as He delivers her from many adversarial actions that manifested during the process of grieving for her son Ilamani of 36 wonderful years.

She can truly relate to God's grace and mercy that He so freely gives to all. While experiencing the after effects of the death of her son, God place this book "In God's Care" to help mend her broken heart. She now has three other books that she is working on and can truly testify that God is omniscience and omnipotence. I say love and peace to my mother Evelyn a true woman of God and who trusts Him no matter what.

Written By: Kenyette Murphy-Wadley

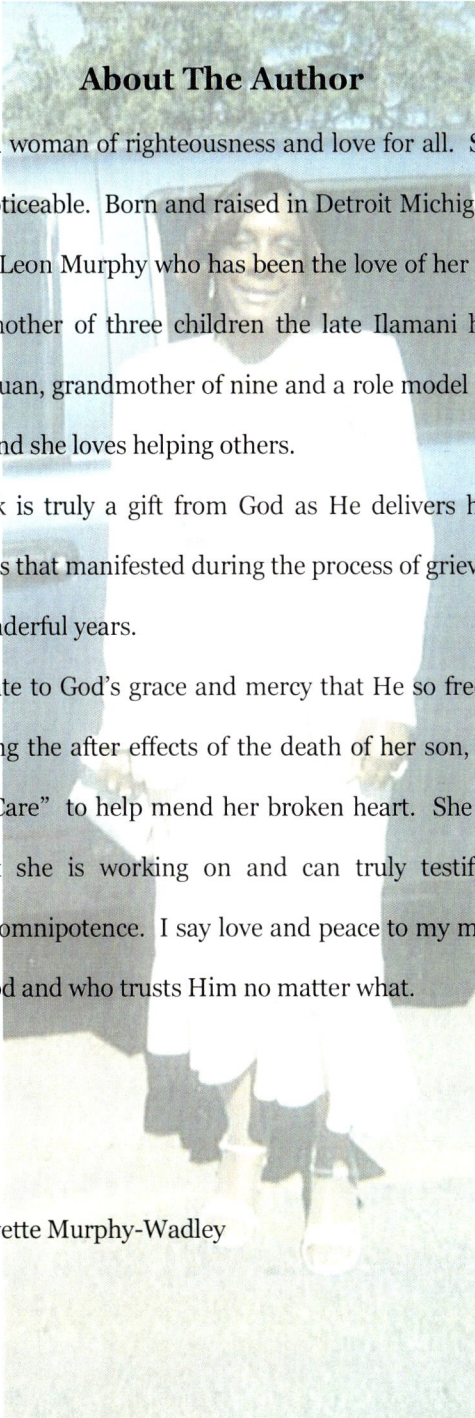

In God's Care